Praise for *Lush*

"Raw, intimate, and brave .... ce
about drinking and addict .... ly
answer) and chronicles C............ journey toward a healing
that at first she can only imagine. Gorgeously written and
audaciously intelligent, here is a controversial and compelling
look at finding your own way back."

—Caroline Leavitt, New York Times bestselling
author of Is This Tomorrow and Pictures of You

"Kerry Cohen applies her legendary wit and sagacity to
women's often subtly destructive dance with alcohol. With
great vulnerability and dynamic prose, Cohen examines her
own descent into the bottle, its ruinous consequences, and her
courageous fight to find her footing in her real life again. This
is a story you won't soon forget."

—Jillian Lauren, New York Times bestselling
memoirist of Some Girls: My Life in a Harem
and Everything You Ever Wanted

"Holy mother of wine—finally a woman wrestles the story of
what it is really like to be a woman away from what we've been
told we are supposed to be. Kerry Cohen's *Lush* will light you
up, crack you up, make you bawl, and most of all, allow you
to breathe again. I'm beyond thrilled to read a book where a
woman tells .... p hole of the
sin-and-red .... redemption.

There's just our lives, and as Cohen reminds us one truth bomb at a time, they are messily gorgeous. Move over, Mary Karr."

—Lidia Yuknavitch, bestselling author of
The Book of Joan and *The Misfit's Manifesto*

"I love this book. I am this book. Kerry Cohen has written a memoir that wrestles with the subtleties, the ambiguities, the sheer alluring horrifying real-life mess of midlife alcohol addiction. For those of us wrestling with demons—and who isn't?—*Lush* is a solace as powerful as red wine."

—Claire Dederer, bestselling author of
Poser: My Life in Twenty-Three Yoga Poses

"Kerry Cohen has hit on something important that's rarely discussed—how the everyday disappointment of middle age can lead to abuses one never imagined as a teenager. Her voice bristles with both vulnerability and sass; her observations and analyses are razor sharp. This is about drinking, but also about the simple anguish of being human. I guzzled *Lush* in one long gulp."

Karen Karbo, author of *The Gospel According to Coco Chanel* and *How Georgia Became O'Keeffe*

"A sharp-eyed look at what it means to be a midlife female unable to cope with either personal demons or the heavy external social pressures placed on women. An intimate and unsparing book of self-reflection."

—*Kirkus Reviews*

Lush

Also by Kerry Cohen

Loose Girl
Seeing Ezra
Dirty Little Secrets
Girl Trouble

Lush

A MEMOIR

Kerry Cohen

sourcebooks

Published by Sourcebooks, Inc.
P.O. Box 4410, Naperville, Illinois 60567-4410
(630) 961-3900
Fax: (630) 961-2168
sourcebooks.com

Library of Congress Cataloging-in-Publication Data

Names: Cohen, Kerry, author.
Title: Lush : a memoir / Kerry Cohen.
Description: Naperville, Illinois : Sourcebooks, [2018]
Identifiers: LCCN 2017061766
Subjects: LCSH: Cohen, Kerry. | Alcoholics--United States--Biography. |
  Alcoholics--Rehabilitation--United States--Biography.
Classification: LCC HV5293.C64 A3 2018 | DDC 362.292092 [B]
--dc23 LC record available at https://lccn.loc.gov/2017061766

Printed and bound in Canada.
MBP 10 9 8 7 6 5 4 3 2

3361408069692790

For my father, with love.

Contents

Lush

Prologue

The Sivananda Ashram Yoga Retreat is situated on Paradise Island, across the bay from Nassau. This is an island lousy with monstrosities for hotels—huge peach-colored castles just down the beach, including the famously extravagant Atlantis. As visitors arrive by boat, wooden signs reassure them that Sivananda is an oasis of tranquility amid the touristy chaos. The retreat is inside a mass of coconut palm trees and bougain-villea and hibiscus, and the foliage is broken up here and there by the small buildings that make up the ashram. There are platforms for yoga classes, a dining area, an open-air temple for *satsang*, a small bookstore with a full library of yogic teachings, and various accommodations for guests, for people staying for karmic residencies, and for people like me, who are here trying to dry out after years of too much drinking.

It's late morning on my first day here, and I'm eating a

brunch of freshly made bread, peanut butter, and yogurt and chatting with two women who are karma yogis. They're living in tents at the ashram for three months and helping with operations, one in reception and one in the kitchen.

I get up and say, "I'm going to get more tea."

"A martini?" one of the women asks.

"More tea," I repeat. "I don't think they serve martinis here."

"Maybe not," she says, "but you can find one five minutes down the beach."

"Noted," I say, and I laugh.

I'm exhausted from traveling, but after brunch, I decide to power through and attend the afternoon yoga class. I end up at the wrong yoga platform and wait long enough to realize I've screwed up. It's too late to join the class, wherever it is, so I walk to the beach and swim in the ocean. The waters of the Caribbean are always a surprise to those of us who live on the West Coast—a turquoise, crystalline blue so thin and sun-shimmering that you can see all the way to the bottom.

I am not unhappy to be missing the yoga class. It's been a decade since I've done yoga, and I am uncomfortably aware of my body. My belly is fat. My arms and shoulders are weak. I don't even want to look at my thighs. Imagine a forty-five-year-old woman who has spent the last five or six years drinking too much wine, smoking cigarettes, and getting little exercise other than sex. My work as a therapist and a writer require me to literally just sit there. That is exactly what I look like. Still, it's not my size that bothers me. It's the fact that I've gone so long without caring for myself in any way. The shame I feel is not about my appearance but about the fact that I've become a drunken lush.

I figure class has let out when I see a few women wandering down to the beach. None are bigger than a size four. There is no mystery about their size, because they're all wearing bikinis. Their skin literally glistens in the sun. I wish I were kidding. Even their posture makes me envious. Despite the research I've conducted about the increase in heavy drinking among middle-aged women, I see little evidence of that trend here. Unless these women metabolize alcohol much differently than I do, they are not drunken lushes.

In Sanskrit, *satsang* means "to be in the company of truth." At Sivananda, *satsang* is when we come together at sunrise and sunset each day, for meditation, chanting, and learning. Doesn't that sound lovely? Even hopeful? But I sit in the wrong place, don't know how to hold my hand during a *pranayama* breathing exercise, and I can't find the right page to follow along with the chanting, known here as *kirtan*. I leave before the final prayer, giving up on the day.

I sprawl in the narrow, hard bed in my tent, the sounds of the party boats from Nassau blaring from the bay. Why have I come here? There are cocktails down the beach at Atlantis, but drinking sounds unappealing for the first time in I can't remember how long. My lack of interest is more upsetting than encouraging, and I wonder if I'll ever find a way to free myself from the daily discomforts of life. This isn't going the way I'd imagined, and if I weren't so bone-tired from frolicking in the Caribbean Sea, I might feel sorry for myself.

I can guess what you're thinking: most people trying to clean up their act don't have the luxury of doing it at some fancy, self-designed rehab in the middle of paradise. So yes, I am an asshole for even thinking this isn't going as well as I'd hoped. But a little more than three years ago, I thought I had everything I wanted, and almost nothing turned out as I'd hoped, and that's why I'm at this ashram in the first place.

When you drink too much, suddenly and seemingly out of nowhere, after a lifetime of little or no drinking, and when you decide one day to finally do something about it after too long not doing anything about it, after wrecking your life in slow, insipid ways you weren't even noticing, you do not want to find that joy is still elusive. You do not want to glamp in the warm, Caribbean air only to find that you're still the asshole who can't feel happy. That was the thing, of course: I couldn't feel happy. That's why I had started drinking too much. Being numb and sloppy was easier than sitting with all the ways my life wasn't what I'd hoped it would have become at this point.

I don't have a story of how I spiraled into alcoholism and then got sober. This is not about how I dropped deep into the darkness of addiction and then saw the light. Instead, I have an unremarkable story, one that many women share but not enough people talk about. It's a story about how I reached midlife, looked around, and thought, *Really? This is how things turned out?* Hit with the reality that so little of what I had imagined would come to be—as a mother, a wife, a woman—I started to drink, and then I started to drink way too much.

I never hit the quintessential "rock bottom," but I know now that I was slowly corroding my life. And the shame I have lived with for as long as I can remember has grown to inordinate proportions, until finally, finally, I am here on this ashram in the middle of goddamn paradise, struggling to find my way through.

One

I wasn't a drunk until I was.

THIS IS THE NON-DRINKING PART OF MY DRINKING STORY.
This is where I tell you about how I didn't drink. I didn't fall
in love with alcohol early in life. It didn't free me from social
anxieties or the fear that I wasn't fun. It didn't give me excuses
to act silly or flirtatious or wild, and I didn't enjoy getting
drunk at parties. I wasn't the first person to arrive or the last
to leave, and I didn't steal alcohol from my parents' liquor
cabinet. And I didn't wind up blacked out or in the ER with
alcohol poisoning.

Here is my short, mostly uneventful history with drinking: When I was eleven, I drank my first sip of alcohol, spiked
cider that my mother made for a Halloween get-together.
The whole house smelled like sweet apples and cinnamon.

My mother's friends stood in the kitchen and on the front stoop, sipping from their cups, unaware of my friend Liz and me hovering nearby, dressed in silvery stockings, our hair pulled into side ponies. We were dressed as "sluts," which was a questionable Halloween trend for girls in the early eighties. Little did I know how fitting that costume would become for the rest of my life.

It was my friend Liz's idea to steal some of the cider. I reached up into the cabinet and got a mug, and I filled it from the stove with the steaming, golden liquid. It tasted good. I felt nothing, having drunk so little, but Liz and I both play-acted that we were drunk, like we'd seen on television.

I didn't drink again until I was thirteen, living with my father and sister in an apartment in Fort Lee, New Jersey. My parents had divorced, and my mother had left us all to go study medicine in the Philippines. My dad was out of town on business and had asked a neighbor to check in on us here and there. My best friend and I threw a party. We invited everyone we knew, and then some older guys got word about the party and showed up too. Someone bought us a whole bunch of Budweiser, and I drank a forty-ouncer, plus one regular can. When Pink Floyd's "Comfortably Numb" came on the stereo, I pressed my ear to the speaker, hugging it like it was speaking directly to me, like it knew me and would care for me. Someone laughed and said, "Oh my God, is she okay?"

The next thing I remember is pushing past all the strangers milling about my apartment on my way to the bathroom, where I threw up. I came out, dizzy and still drunk, and lay on my bed for a little while. A boy I liked, Brian, was in my room, along with a bunch of other kids. They sat on the floor passing a joint. I was planning to woo Brian that night, but he glanced at me without interest when I came in. I tried to position myself on my twin bed, which was adorned with the same Laura Ashley quilt I'd had since I was seven, so that I would look sexy, or at least as sexy as I could look with sunken eyes and a greenish tint to my skin. Brian didn't look my way again until I ran to the bathroom to throw up some more.

By the time the party was over, my dad's drugs were gone from his underwear drawer. So was a handgun I didn't even know he had. Our kitchen was in the middle of a renovation, and we had a bunch of small appliances in boxes and stacks of tiles for the floor. The appliances were gone. Someone had thrown tiles off the terrace. A car's windshield was broken, and the pool covering was ripped. My father wound up with a lawsuit. As punishment, I had to go to work with him, at a company where he was vice president of engineering, for the rest of the summer.

He didn't talk to me about underage drinking or about excessive drinking at any age. He spoke only about the inconvenience I'd caused him.

The lesson that stayed with me was that alcohol hurt my chances of getting what I most wanted: boys. How could I be sexy when I was hugging speakers or vomiting in the bathroom? When I went to parties after that, I'd get a bottle of beer, empty it in a bathroom sink, and fill it with water. Then I'd nurse that bottle the rest of the night.

This nonstory, this lack of history with alcohol, is the reason I grew concerned when I started drinking too much in my forties. Before that, I had just one relentless addiction: boys. Boys were my drug—their dark eyes, their hands, the way the whole world disappeared when the ones I liked turned their gaze to me, put their arms around me, opened my legs. Addicts talk about the first time they did their drug, The One, that would become their lifelong weakness. They talk about how right away it was like an answer: *yes, this is what I've been looking for.* Boys were my salvation in the same way, my elixir of choice, my heroin. I believed they would save me from my pain. I was wrong, of course. And as with other drug addictions, I ruined everything in my life trying to get that salvation, until I finally had to change my ways.

I used boys to keep myself out of relationships, and when I got into relationships, I used them to keep a foot out the door. It took me a long time to understand that, in my early forties, I was using drinking to do the same thing. When you spend years recovering from one addiction, even making it part of your life's work, other addictions are likely to creep in. A therapy client of mine once described it as squeezing a water balloon: when you squeeze one part down, another bulge pops out somewhere else.

My new bulge was filled with wine, because once you're in your forties, it seems as if everyone is drinking. Have you noticed this? When you're in your twenties, it seems everyone is drinking because they're young and immortal and have no responsibilities. In your thirties, everyone stops for a bit to have babies. And suddenly in your forties, you can't swing a yoga mat without hitting a woman guzzling merlot.

One night, I was at a party with a small group of women I had never met before, and we were talking about how we sometimes unintentionally drank more than we thought we should. All of us were in our early forties, except one woman's mother. The mother said, "When I get together with my friends, we share three or four bottles."

"Of course, it's just you and one other woman," I joked.

We all laughed. "Actually, it's usually just three of us."

We nodded, mentally calculating the number of glasses per woman.

A tall woman with short, auburn hair said, "I feel awful those nights I drink a whole bottle. I'll think to myself that I didn't drink the whole thing, but then I see the bottle the next day, and there's this much left." She gestured with her fingers to show about an eighth of an inch. Again, we all nodded.

The mother said, "And you don't really feel awful that night. It's the next day you feel so bad."

More nods.

None of us questioned *why* we were suddenly drinking in this way.

I may not have been alone with my budding habit, but already I worried mine was more alarming, if only because I hadn't been a drinker before. I had started to drink too much too often, and I was doing so because I was increasingly unhappy with what was happening in my life. I had been so sure I'd conquered my issues with men, and now here I was in what was shaping up to be yet another shitty relationship with yet another man who couldn't love me. After everything I'd been through, I didn't want to accept the possibility of another loss. Instead of facing that fear, I drank, because wine helped me tamp down all the awful, painful feelings I lived with every day.

Grown-ups drink wine, right? It was classy to drink a glass of pinot noir over dinner, to pop open a bottle when guests arrived. Before I drank regularly, I had a fantasy of myself in a silk robe, floating down a sweeping staircase, holding—you guessed it—a glass of wine. For all the ways I'd fucked up adulthood, a glass of wine seemed almost like an accomplishment. Until, of course, it became one more thing I took too far.

Two

I have a hole.

I DID NOT BECOME A LUSH OVERNIGHT. IT CREPT UP ON ME without warning over the course of several years. Because I had watched people in my family struggle with drugs, adultery, self-involvement, and a certain carelessness with other people's feelings, I knew I needed to be wary of those behaviors in my own life. And I was guilty of all those things over time and to varying degrees. But alcoholism? I knew of no one near my branch of the family tree who had struggled with that. First of all, we were Jews, and Jews are not known for their alcohol use, aside from the Manischewitz in our glasses on high holidays. In fact, there is evidence that 20 percent of all Jews carry a genetic mutation that helps to protect against alcoholism.* Thanks to my awareness of this biological fluke, I had not lived as many of my friends had, closely watching their behavior with alcohol because maybe they had Irish blood and knew of the cultural stereotype or they had grown up with alcoholic parents.† For them, alcohol seemed like a predator waiting to pounce. For me, it was just a casual acquaintance I enjoyed seeing on occasion.

Before my parents divorced, they had cocktail parties in the big front yard of our house in Harrington Park, New Jersey. My sister and I danced and twirled to the music—the Rolling Stones and Fleetwood Mac—before my mother shuffled us off to bed. I'd lie there, too wound up to sleep, and listen to the songs and the murmur of conversations, the pricks of high-pitched laughter. I loved those nights. Something about knowing my parents were just outside with their friends and that everyone was having fun made me feel safe. No one was throwing up or crying. I wouldn't wake up to find one of my parents' friends passed out in the front yard. They were happy, which meant they would be there if I needed them. My parents' happiness together revolved around nights like this. Decades later, when talking about their marriage, my father

Kerry Cohen

---

* David Derbyshire, "Gene Helps Jews Resist Alcoholism," *Telegraph*, September 17, 2002, http://www.telegraph.co.uk/news/science/science-news/3299335/Gene-helps-Jews-resist-alcoholism.html.

† For a full study of alcoholism and heritability, see D. M. Dick and L. J. Bierut, "The Genetics of Alcohol Dependence," *Current Psychiatry Reports* 8, no. 2 (2006): 151–157.

told me, "You can say what you want about your mother, but those days were fun, and that was due to her."

After the divorce, my dad rolled joints and kept them in his Marlboro Lights pack. He smoked them in his car, and he smoked them in his room, and sometimes he smoked them around the apartment when my sister and I were there. By that time, my mother had moved away to attend medical school, and we lived with my father. His closet was filled with paper grocery bags that were packed full of Ziploc bags of pot. There must have been eight pounds of weed in there. I had no idea why he needed so much.

He collected pills—Percocet, Percodan, and Vicodin. I didn't know how he got the pills, but I did know where he kept them: in the back of his bathroom cabinet. He told me once how they made you feel. He said that they didn't take away the pain, but they made it so you didn't give a shit about it. He also kept rolled-up dollar bills in his underwear drawer, along with a large bag of cocaine. He worked harder to hide that.

I didn't know when my father was stoned. I didn't know if he was funnier or spacier or hungrier or more of a contemplator. As far as I knew, my father was always stoned. He was always off in his head, thinking about heat transfer and valves and energy efficiency. He designed water heaters for a living, and he was obsessed with his work. Sometimes he drew illustrations in the air with his fingers. Other times he paced back and forth, thinking, seemingly unable to hear me when I called for him.

I have no idea when he did coke. Nor do I know when

he took those pills. Maybe even he recognized that there were some lines he shouldn't cross.

At fourteen, I smoked his pot regularly. My friend and I cut school, got high, and lay on my floor while we listened to Pink Floyd albums. Later, as a senior in high school and in college, I did cocaine too. During my late teens and early twenties, it was my drug of choice, but it was expensive and awkward to snort, and I never felt comfortable doing hard drugs like that. It just wasn't who I wanted to be. I tried those pills a few times too. Indeed, they did just what my father had said. A friend once told me that the few times she was prescribed drugs after oral surgery, she hoarded them, because physical pain was tolerable; it was emotional pain that so often felt unbearable. So very true. But pills were hard to get too, and I was a person who had always been careful about doing too much of a drug I liked. Perhaps, like children of alcoholics, I was vigilant about my drug use, careful not to fall down any holes.

Throughout my teenage years, my mother called every Sunday. I didn't want to talk to her. I liked to pretend I didn't have a mother. All I had to do was simply not mention her, forget her as best I could, and the pain of the fact that she left me wouldn't sting. The reality of her absence snuck in, though, no matter how hard I tried to pretend I didn't care that she wasn't in my life. Once, a friend said, "Why do you always defend your mother? She left you!" My chest caved in. *She left you.* I didn't like to think of it. I didn't like to be reminded. I believed in my whole body that she left because I was unlovable.

When she called, I said as little as possible. My sister took care of our mother's need to be connected, but I refused to give anything. I answered in monosyllabic words. *Yes. Fine. Okay. Bye.*

"I love you," she always said.

I said nothing back.

Years later, I'd watch the Albert Brooks film *Mother*. Debbie Reynolds, playing Brooks's mom, says on the phone, "Okay, honey. I love you." He says, "I know you think you do."

I had no sense of what it would be like to feel loved. I ached for it, and every moment was filled with that ache. My eyes were constantly on the lookout for a boy who would help ease that pain. This feeling of being unlovable became its own addiction over time. And that's the core of my story. It's about how drugs and alcohol were not a problem in my past and how much the absence of my parents' love was. It's about how I learned to escape but not initially with alcohol. When my mother and father were too caught up in their own needs to care about mine, I went outside—literally, to the streets, where men drove by in cars or passed on the sidewalk—to find the attention I wanted. I spent my adolescence and twenties doing whatever I could to lose myself in men. I swam around in the fantasy of them. I handed them my sadness, saying, "Here, you take this. Here, you make me feel better."

That pain of feeling unlovable. I knew it so well—the familiar cushion of its hurt, the soft, forgiving pity of it. As my belief in my inability to be loved became part of my identity,

I came to rely on it to know who I was. When men did love me, it wasn't enough. I couldn't feel it. *I know you think you do.* My precious emptiness was like a shield against love. I pushed men away with that shield and then sobbed, "See? No one can love me! I am simply unlovable!"

Still, I had yet to find escape in drinking. In my twenties, my grandparents poured my boyfriend and me glasses of $250 wine. I couldn't taste what was so great about it. Years later, of course, I was much more interested. The labels were so pretty. All those foreign words and artistic images. Those labels alone made me feel like a more interesting person, like maybe something exciting was about to unfold. And then the taste of the wine, its body and boldness and mouthfeel. Mouthfeel! Good wine inspires words like "mouthfeel"!

When I visited my mother in Chicago, her husband always opened a bottle first thing, and then he and I went out onto the balcony where I smoked cigarettes and he smoked a cigar. My mother hated that. But inevitably, as the evening progressed, she'd get slurry and wet-eyed and emotional, and we'd be able to connect in ways we never could before we drank together.

One night, I said, "You're drunk."

With a look of disgust at my boorish suggestion, she answered, "You cannot get drunk on good wine."

But once, she fell into the bushes behind my house after we had been drinking good wine all night. So, um, yes, you can.

A few times, when we drank together, she let me know

how hard those years were, back when I was a kid, how terri-fied she was that she had made the wrong choice. She has never said the words, "I'm sorry." The tears were about her *own* loss, *her* guilt. Her regret was about leaving us with our father, as opposed to giving up our relationship. But that was the best she could do. And it meant something to me that she knew this was the pressure point between us, that this was the thing we would both carry to our graves. She would always have abandoned me, and I would always have been abandoned. It was a connection we would always share.

My father had a different way of escaping. His approach involved substances, for sure. But he also avoided difficult conversations. He got annoyed when I had feelings of any kind—except anger. Anger was acceptable, so we shared a lot of that. My father's standard line was, "Check, please!" If someone happened to have an emotion, he wanted out of there right away.

Both my parents left, you see, and in their places, they left a hole.

Somewhere inside me is that hole.

It isn't a real hole, of course. But my God, sometimes it feels like an actual thing, an absence and lack, the way I imagine a hole would feel. That is what my parents left me: a hole. And I have spent my life trying to fill it. I've been in therapy since I was nineteen years old. I have examined this hole from all sides, analyzing it like a scientist, also feeling it so intensely that the pain took the shape of waves, washing over me, drowning me, not letting me breathe. I still feel this pain regularly. I am both the woman who bears that hole and the hole itself. And *this*, this is the real source of my addiction story, of my drinking story, of every story I have to tell.

Three

I was a consolation prize.

I BELIEVE THAT EVERYONE YOU MEET SHOWS YOU WHO THEY really are in the first one or two weeks of knowing them. On Bob's and my second date, he kissed me passionately, and in that kiss, I could feel the desperation of a man who had not kissed passionately for far too long. In those first months, most of what we did was drink and fuck. We were both recently separated from our first spouses, and we both still lived with them, so we did a lot of fucking in our Priuses with our kids' car seats fastened in the back seats. At that point, I was not drinking excessively. I was not yet a lush.

My first marriage, to Michael, began with hope and excitement. I had finally found a wonderful man who loved me, who was fun and funny and kind. Then we had babies, and our first son had special needs. We lost money on houses. Work was stressful, and family lived far away. Eventually, we didn't want to have sex with each other anymore. We looked at each other and thought, "You're always here; you must be the reason I'm unhappy." Michael and I decided to separate, but we continued to live together. We drank wine in the evenings, after the kids had gone to bed, and we sat outside so we could smoke. We shared a bottle, processing the end of our marriage. We were not belligerent drunks. We were nice drunks. Fun drunks. We liked to have a good time, and we hadn't stopped liking each other. I lived with him for a year and a half after we separated, and those evening talks over wine made that enjoyable. In fact, this is when we became good friends.

I was thirty-nine and not a drunk yet, but I still felt that old familiar tug of male attention. I didn't have to look far. I had been having a kind of emotional affair during my marriage with a man I'd met before Michael. We had stayed in touch. Did I mention I have intimacy issues? Clearly, there was never a time I was good at love. As my marriage began its downturn, things between this man and me heated up, though we'd never been physical. Two weeks after Michael and I officially separated, I arranged to meet him. We had sex, finally, and it was disappointing. Maybe there was too much buildup. Maybe we weren't compatible in bed. But also, in the nine years I'd known him and thought I was in love with him, he hadn't changed a bit. He was still indecisive about his marriage and me and what he wanted, and I was heading somewhere new. Michael and I were getting out of our rut, and the last thing I wanted was to stand still again. I decided not to see him anymore. Instead, I was going to have *good* sex! So I did exactly that, with seventeen men over the course of the next year and a half, ending with Bob, who was just two weeks into his own separation.

Recounting any relationship is a game of *he said, she said*. When it ends badly, when it was too often heightened with emotion, and when at least one of us was drunk a lot of the time, it's hard to say who has the accurate account. I know for sure Bob would disagree with almost everything I'll say here about how it happened and who did what.

This is the *she said*. This is my story as best I can recall.

The evening before I moved into my own house, Michael and I shared a bottle of wine. It was a July night, right before our older son, Ezra, would turn seven. We sat in the backyard, under an expanse of stars. I loved that house, and I was going to miss it. It was a ranch that had been updated with modernist touches. It had big windows that let the rooms fill with natural light. The master suite in the basement had a bathroom almost as big as the bedroom. There were two square sinks, a huge tub, a stand-up shower, and heated floors. God, I loved that bathroom. And the kitchen had a beautiful tile backsplash and large slate tiles on the floor, new stainless-steel appliances, and windowed wooden cabinets.

But the truth of our relationship lived in that house too. I'd coerced Michael into buying it even though we couldn't sell the old one, and we were in a financial crisis that was

Lush

23

largely my fault. His resentment over that was palpable, and I'd been sleeping with our younger son, Griffin, in the master while Michael slept with Ezra. Before we developed this new friendship, we hardly had real conversations unless they were about parenting logistics.

Now, he said, "Maybe you shouldn't go. Maybe we can figure this out."

I looked up at the sky, at the stars thick and heavy in the pale black. I took a drag of my cigarette. I was in love with Bob by then. I didn't look at Michael.

"I'm sorry," I told him.

I suspect he may have kept going in our numb, deadened marriage, not because he was happy, but because he had gotten used to being unhappy. The decision to end our marriage was mutual, but I moved out because one of us had to do it, and it might as well be me. I simply added the final punctuation to our split.

Bob and Michael helped me move into my new house, which was Michael's and my old house, the one we hadn't been able to sell. I don't like to think back to those first weeks. Michael and I started Ezra and Griffin on a schedule they'd eventually become familiar with, but it was terribly confusing for them at first. One week with me, and one week with Michael. I timed it so that Bob and I had our kids at the same time, so our weeks without kids coincided.

Ezra cried and said he wanted to go home to Daddy. He and I lay together on his bed while I held his sobbing body. He'd always been a Daddy's boy, and while I knew he loved me, Daddy was his favorite. "I know, baby," I said softly. "I know."

I didn't drink every night. When my kids were there, I focused only on them. I spent so many hours lying with them in bed, being with the animal core of them as we went through this change. During those weeknights without them, though, I sat on my front stoop with a bottle of red wine, a glass, and a pack of all-natural, ultralight, "earth-friendly" American Spirits—you know, cigarettes that are good for you and the planet. After all those nights of drinking and smoking with Michael, it had become a harmless habit that helped me unwind.

Bob and I had the kind of connection that starts at the top of your skull and goes all the way to your toes. We were drawn to each other relentlessly. If we were in the same room, you could feel the electricity. One of my friends told me that being around us made *her* horny. And it wasn't just sexual. It was everything. We communicated intensely and constantly. We were both writers, and we shared not only that community, but also a love of reading and a certain way of thinking about the world. The whole thing felt so...*significant*.

For my fortieth birthday, Bob planned a romantic getaway to Belknap Hot Springs, about an hour and a half east of Eugene, Oregon. He reserved a house that had a redwood hot tub with a view of the McKenzie River, which is one of our many beautiful rivers in Oregon. We spent the weekend doing my three favorite things: writing, talking, and fucking. We drank a lot, because drinking had become part of our routine now. Wine lubricated our conversations and enhanced our already fiery libidos.

I had asked Bob to move in with me, and he was thinking about it. He said yes, and then no, and then yes again. This back-and-forth, this jolting, nauseating movement of his feelings about me, about us, would inform the pattern and shape of our relationship. It hurt, but it seemed reasonable, especially so early on. He hadn't been on his own after he and his wife separated. His wife had asked for the split, and two weeks later, he asked me on a date. Our connection had been so powerful and bursting with electricity that he hadn't dated anyone else, or been alone, or figured out what he wanted. His uncertainty was reasonable, but in the narrative of my life, it poked hard at my basic pain, my feelings of worthlessness.

Every few months, I sensed that Bob was distancing himself from me, which I assumed was because he figured he should be alone. I'd drop into my despair about being unlovable, and he would say that he loved me and didn't want to lose me, and I'd feel chosen again.

If you want to make a love addict all yours, if you want her to become compulsively attached to you, this is what you do. You bind her inside a process of partial reinforcement. You withdraw again and again without warning, and then, when you think she might finally be ready to leave, you give her what she needs. Do this often enough, and she'll be too broken to consider leaving ever again. I don't believe Bob did this intentionally. I don't believe he had a master plan. Still, he had unwittingly trapped me, and I couldn't escape. And through all of it, we drank. We drank when he pulled away, and we drank when he came closer. We drank when I was in pain, and we drank when I was happy. We drank when we talked things through, and we drank when we came back together.

And then there was his house, which he loved and didn't want to leave, even though it was too small for our new family of six, which we would be every other week. His house was a little Portland bungalow in the Alberta Arts district, a gentrified, exceedingly hip area, full of coffeehouses, restaurants, bars, and boutiques. His house was within walking distance of events like Last Thursday, which showcases local artists' work, and I knew he loved that he could walk to all these things that represented so much of Portland's chicness.

Bob's love for his house seemed to somehow parallel his love for his ex-wife, which I believed he still felt. I told him many times I felt like a consolation prize, but this wasn't just about Bob. I had spent my life feeling like a consolation prize. My parents seemed put upon by my need for them to show their love with more than words, in a way that I might actually feel. Every boy who said he loved me did so because I cajoled him into a relationship, and then I was simply the default girl to love, or that's how it felt to me. Even Michael, the one who married me, the one who truly loved me, had grown emotionally unavailable.

I went into the relationship with my love addiction freshly broken open, which wasn't a great way to start. But Bob had his own issues too, mostly about his attraction to other women. And nothing, absolutely *nothing*, triggered my feelings of low self-worth more than other women. The first was someone he'd met at his MFA program. She was beautiful, dark-skinned, and living in another country. As we drove out to a house I'd rented on the coast for Valentine's Day, he told me they had exchanged emails, because why not drop that bit of truth on me right before our romantic weekend?

The second was a lovely writer we met together, a woman who was excited to meet me because she was a fan of *Loose Girl*. I was still naive about this inclination of his, so I was surprised when he told me, on a flight to a writing conference, that she had sent him her phone number when he asked on Facebook if anyone wanted to meet up there.

I didn't know what was going on in these women's minds. They probably didn't intend to provoke his desire, but that didn't matter. What bothered me was what was in Bob's mind. He was thinking about them, imagining being with them. He was unsure about me and wanted to see what else was out there, as if I were a kind of cheese. *I like cheddar fine, but let's see what else you have on the menu.* I ordered a glass of wine from the flight attendant.

There are women out there who would never tolerate what I did, what I've always tolerated when it comes to men. The minute a man becomes uncertain about them, the minute he admits to thinking he shouldn't be there, they leave. They pack their shit and get the fuck out. They know they deserve better. Or maybe they know that if they act like they deserve better, they will receive better. I had never been that person. I didn't leave men. If I did leave, it was over a long, sticky, tortured period. I was always too sad, too hurt, too lost when it came to love.

Because Bob and I were both writers, I foolishly held onto a notion of us as being like Joan Didion and John Gregory Dunne as she described their relationship before he died. They wrote together and read paragraphs to one another as they did, sharing feedback. We liked to get out of town as often as possible to write. Even though my career had faltered since *Loose Girl*, my first memoir, it had not disintegrated. I was still selling books, albeit not for nearly as much money, so I was always busy working on the next one. Bob was always working on something too. Most often, we went to the Oregon coast, where one of his friends had a vacation home. The northern Oregon coast is made up of windswept bluffs making way for dark-green woods of firs and ferns. The ocean was cold and rough. And in this particular section of the coast, wild bunnies hopped anywhere there was grass. We brought food, so we didn't have to leave the house, and we got busy writing. It's hard to remember now after everything that happened, but we did like each other once. We had thoughtful conversations and a shared sense of humor, and we were crazy for each other physically.

Drinking wine on the deck at that house, he told me he had another crush. I knew about her. I knew he had been in contact with her. I knew they had some things in common, things that held no interest for me. She loved to exercise. She played Magic: The Gathering, or whatever. And she did not drink a lot or smoke cigarettes.

Perhaps this is a good place to mention that Bob drank and smoked too, even more than I did at times. But he wanted to stop, you see, and he said he couldn't do that unless I did it with him, which I wasn't ready to do. Most of our time together still included drinking, and when we drank, we sat in our backyard, or in a bar somewhere, or in this beach house on the Oregon coast. We talked about our relationship—a lot. My friend Naomi once suggested Bob and I shared too much with each other. "Why does he have to tell you everything he's thinking?" she asked. But I didn't want to be kept from anything he was thinking, and this oversharing had become a part of the fabric of our relationship. It may have been unhealthy, but I'd convinced myself I'd rather know than not. And drinking often made hearing his thoughts a little less painful, because Bob, unlike any man I'd ever been with, wanted me to know him wholly, to know who he was.

That night, he wanted me to know he had feelings for this woman.

"What does that mean, you have feelings for her?" I asked, the pain a knot in my throat.

"I want to be honest with you," he said.

"Do you want to be with her instead?"

"I'm not saying that."

"Then what? What *are* you saying?" I could hear the pitch of my voice, which had risen, but I couldn't seem to stop it.

"I'm struggling." He didn't look at me. "I wish you'd be more understanding."

"*You're* struggling?" I stood up, wobbling as I did. I grabbed my glass of wine and my pack of cigarettes and opened the sliding glass door. I lurched through the house, the tears uncontrollable. I went back outside through the front door, sat against the side of the house, and lit a cigarette. I wanted to believe this issue of his would go away. I had to. It was so hard to reconcile the electric connection we had, the fun and laughter, with his inability to be entirely with me and only me. I was not enough for him, not right for him, and yet I believed him when he said he didn't want to lose me.

It is hard to not want to go back there and shake my shoulders, hold my face in my own hands, and tell myself what I needed to hear. *This will not get better. This relationship will chip away at your spirit. You will become a drunk. You will hurt children in the process. It will end badly, and there will be no winners.* But we can rarely save ourselves from the bad choices we've made.

In the morning, we woke hungover and emotionally exhausted. "It's time to make some changes," he said. This would become a refrain over time. He meant how much we drank and nothing more. But that wouldn't get better either.

It must have been hard for people close to me to understand why I kept trying. I kept trying because this was my second time around. I kept trying because I feared this would be my last chance, not just for love but for feeling hopeful about love. *But that's not how it went*, Bob told me. *You tried because you loved me.* I suppose that's true too.

I moved into my house in July, and Bob joined me in

October. He thought maybe if he just did it, he'd be more resolved. He loved me. He didn't want to lose me. It seemed like the correct thing to do, he told me. When he first arrived, with his two children—an eight-year-old girl and a three-year-old boy—I wondered if all this pushing for us to live together might have been a mistake. His children's energy was so different from my own children's. They couldn't stop moving their bodies. They ran through the house. They had no sense of personal space, no impulse control. I felt like I had to wear armor, to protect myself every moment with them.

This is difficult to admit, because it sounds so insensitive. They're just children, after all. But the terrible truth is I didn't like having them around. I dreaded their arrival, even as I craved my own children's. Had Bob and I not been engaged in our shitty cycle of go-away-come-closer, we might have noticed that our families weren't going to blend well. It was the first of many things we did that hurt our children during this time.

One afternoon when my kids weren't there and his were, I was so desperate, so confused by my frustration, that I left the house and took a walk. When I came home, Bob asked, "Did you leave because of my children?" What could I say? The answer was yes. But I couldn't say that, and it scared the shit out of me. I washed down my fear and guilt with a couple of glasses of wine.

My friends stood by, wide-eyed and concerned. "Kerry," they said carefully, "we just want to make sure you've thought this relationship through."

"I *know*," I answered, annoyed. "I'm not an idiot."

I was in love with Bob. I believed we had a future together, and because I was happy—or some version of happy—I was replacing my addiction to boys with a growing addiction to wine. I was pushing down the love part of my addiction balloon, and the new bulge was filled with wine! Maybe drinking helped quiet reservations I might have had about Bob otherwise. But it would be fine. Once we smoothed out the wrinkles in our relationship, I would simply drink less.

Addiction specialists say that everyone has either a problematic relationship to alcohol, a controlled relationship to alcohol, or no relationship to alcohol. For most of my life, I'd had no relationship. It did nothing for me. But now? Now wine was doing something for me, but it wasn't a problem. Not yet.

I told Bob when we were first together, in those luxurious throes of love when everything felt possible, that there were exactly two things I needed, and everything else was negligible. I said, "I need to feel loved entirely, and I need you to desire me sexually. That's it."

At the time, after separating from a woman who had seemed endlessly frustrated with his inability to make enough money, with his messiness in their house, with all sorts of things that had made him feel inadequate, he said, "That's so easy."

But it wasn't. Loving one person entirely is not always so easy.

Four

I wanted to be better.

WHEN BOB AND I WERE FIRST TOGETHER, I DRANK ONLY when I was with him or with friends, and I had plenty of friends. My dysfunctional family of origin was a bust, and for as long as I can remember, I have built makeshift families with friends. I am forever on the lookout for people to *belong* to, and over time, my ability to create "friend groups" has become something of an art. I am what is called a connector. I make friends easily, and then I get them together, and voilà! We become a group of friends that feels like an extended family but without the misery.

My closest friends then were Julia, Naomi, and Lauren.

Julia was my first friend who had an autistic child, like I did. Our kids went to the same school, and we met one afternoon when we were picking them up. The teachers were raving about her son. They told her what a great job he'd done that day, how hard he'd worked, and how well he was doing. Fed up with his behavior at home, she said, "He can go fuck himself." Right then, I knew we'd be friends. I loved her irreverent humor and how she was willing to say the things I felt. Having a child with special needs presents a different set of struggles from what parents of neurotypical kids face. Our children are not welcomed. They are teased and belittled, slapped with labels, and tossed into boxes that don't necessarily fit. The pain we share in our love for our children and the singular grief that comes with that love means more to me than anything. It always will.

When I first met Naomi, I felt as if I'd found a piece of home. When you live in a city like Portland where there are maybe a dozen Jews and you find one from New York? You don't let them out of your sight, even when you're from Jersey. I loved her emotional intelligence and her understanding of people and relationships. She had no time for bullshit. She did, however, make time to hang out with me on patios and watch me drink, and she didn't judge me when I smoked cigarette after cigarette. But Naomi didn't smoke, and she rarely got drunk. Instead, she usually left early to go home to her husband and daughter.

Lauren and I had mutual girlfriends, and Bob and I were friends with her then-boyfriend. We first met at a local wine bar with a group of people. When I said I was going outside to have a cigarette, she jumped up to join me, because smokers are always relieved to find someone else with that disgusting habit. We were both divorced moms, and we were both dating men with their first marriages behind them and a lot of commitment issues ahead. Our friendship started as we stood on the sidewalk outside the bar, cigarettes between our fingers, swapping stories most people might not share the first time they meet someone.

Whatever is going on in my life, I've found girlfriends who enjoyed and needed the same things I did. In my twenties, I commiserated with single friends over the joys of dating. In my thirties, my friends and I were moms with new babies, and we talked a lot about how little sleep we got. In my forties, I happened to start hanging out with women who drank. Have you heard that maxim that everyone comes into your life for a reason? Well, I seem to unconsciously bring people into my life for my own reasons.

My fortysomething girlfriends and I talked, and we laughed. We had fun, my friends and I. We were *funny*. I needed that humor and entertainment more than anything. Because we all drank, sometimes excessively, it felt perfectly normal to me then—more normal than watering down a beer to nurse all night. I was loosening up in a whole new way! We had children in elementary school, and holidays like Fourth of July and Easter and Mother's Day were more fun when we were all together, talking and laughing and, yes, drinking and smoking. Hell, any day was more fun when we were doing that. The children were having their own fun, just being kids together. We left the men in charge, and we took a break from worrying.

Bob hated this setup. He said it was bad parenting, so while the other dads took over, Bob stayed home. What he really meant, as far as I can tell, was that it was bad *mothering*, and he had no interest in picking up my slack.

At first, there were times my girlfriends and I met for coffee. At first, we focused on food and conversation. But over time, we ended up enabling each other's bad habits until wine permeated almost everything we did. We didn't do yoga together. We didn't meet for mani-pedis or to go shopping or whatever other women do. We met for drinks. We had drinks in someone's backyard, or at a bar, or at a restaurant with a decent (but inexpensive) house red and an outdoor patio for smoking.

Despite all the ways Bob judged my behavior—as a mother, with alcohol and cigarettes, as a housekeeper, as a social person who "held court" (his words)—he must have wanted our relationship to work as much as I did. He must have been just as afraid as I was that this could be our last chance, because we talked regularly about marriage.

In late spring, Bob set up a fancy dinner at a restaurant he knew I liked. We shared a bottle of wine with the meal, and afterward, he took me for a walk along the waterfront of the Willamette River. Portland's downtown skyline was on the other side. It was a clear night with stars dotting the sky. The water lapped gently at the rocks below the promenade where we walked. He guided me to a bench, and there he produced a ring, along with a folded piece of paper.

"Read it," he said.

I read it. He had handwritten a letter to me while on a camping trip with a couple of friends. It said, in a poetic way, that I had provided a soft landing for him after his marriage fell apart and that I'd been there for him when he was upset. I pushed away the sinking feeling that he had written only about what I'd done for him and nothing about me as a person who was lovable for reasons that did not involve him.

I said yes.

I would like to say we started planning our wedding filled with glee and enthusiasm about our future, but that is not how things went at all. We planned an engagement brunch and invited all our friends. In reality, I planned the party alone in my ongoing effort to make this relationship we were having mimic a good idea. I bought a cute dress to wear. Naomi brought good bagels and cream cheese and fancy salmon in chafing dishes. Chafing dishes!

That morning, Bob was surly, and he said, "Why should I be excited about your friends coming over?" even though I had invited his friends too. We argued, because who doesn't argue right before their engagement party? It was a beautiful spread and a beautiful day, but when our guests arrived, I was pissed off and halfway into a bottle of wine. I spent most of the day outside, drinking and smoking with my friends. Bob and I barely went near each other during that party, the party meant to celebrate our love and our future lives together.

Less than a month later, I took the ring off my finger. "Give it back to me when you're actually ready," I said.

I knew he wasn't ready.

In early autumn, Bob was invited to a three-week writing retreat on the Oregon coast. I drove out Route 6 one night to join him for a week. The drive to the coast is beautiful, and it felt so romantic. The dense, leafy forest. My headlights dim on the winding road. The silence in the car. Belle and Sebastian weather. When I got there, we had wild sex. We always did. He held my face in his hands and said, "I love you, I love you, I love you."

We wrote during the day. We drove to the water, and we took a canoe across the way to an island. No one there. Just rocks and sky and water. In the evening, I drank and slipped out to the porch to smoke. It was that night, after we had sex, that I opened the nightstand drawer. I don't know what I was looking for, but my intentions were innocent. In that drawer, I found a strip of condoms. We didn't use condoms. What did he need condoms for? He came out of the bathroom, and I asked him why he had condoms.

"What?" he asked.

"Condoms," I repeated. "There are condoms in your drawer."

"I don't know," he said.

"You don't know?"

"I don't know."

He didn't know.

He figured it out soon enough. He'd thrown old condoms in his bag. He had put them in the nightstand when he got there. He had done so unwittingly, but he knew that didn't excuse it. He was open to something other than us, other than me. He was screwed up. He was sorry. He didn't know. *He didn't know.*

I lay in bed, my eyes wide. At some point, I got up, poured another glass of wine, and sat outside with a cigarette. The wine warmed my body. It was a friend by now, patting my back. *It's okay. It will all be okay.* It slid into my veins, into the soft tissue of my heart. Wine made me better. It made Bob better in my mind, and it made our relationship okay.

But it wasn't okay. I wanted to be Bob's first choice. Just once, I wanted to be *someone's* first choice. Lauren once said to me, "We're no one's first choice anymore." She meant because we were middle-aged. She meant because we generally dated men who were divorced from their first (or second or third) wives. She meant that the time for first choices was over. Was I such a romantic fool to think I could have that now?

Still, I wasn't ready to give up on Bob, and I wasn't ready to quit having fun with my friends.

In the summer, Julia's yard exploded with color. There was a huge playground set, a garden full of lettuce and tomatoes and peas, and a thick green lawn. Julia was the opposite of me when it came to domesticity. She was good at it. So was her husband, Mitch. We all spent many hours at their house, usually with kids.

The yard had a bubbling fountain that overflowed into a pond. It was pretty, but in late spring and early summer, the tadpoles had grown into frogs, and their croaking was as loud as locusts. One spring night, when we could hardly hear ourselves talk, Julia stood by the edge of the pond and screamed at the frogs. "Shut the fuck up! Shut! The! Fuck! Up!" The rest of us giggled.

Lauren stepped onto one of the rocks in the pond to see if she could catch one. "I'm stuck," she said. "Help?"

We laughed again.

"I'll get you," I said, and I tottered over with my wineglass and reached for her hand. She took it, and as she pulled, I lost my footing and fell. My jaw hit one of Julia's planter pots. I sat on the ground, stunned.

"Oh my God! Are you okay?" Everyone gathered around, and someone helped me up.

Lauren said, "You're still holding your glass. It probably didn't even spill."

Sure enough, my glass was firmly in my grasp, unbroken. But it had spilled. Most of the red wine was on my linen pants and pale shirt. (Over time, all my clothes and shoes would come to have wine stains.)

My jaw thumped with pain, but otherwise I felt okay.

I caught a ride home with Lauren and her (now) husband. I texted Bob that I was on my way, but he didn't respond.

"What the fuck?" he said when he saw me, and I told him what happened.

"I'm having fun!" I said. "God forbid you ever have fun too!"

He shook his head, but I wasn't done. My friends' husbands often hung out with us when we drank. Even

Michael did, strange as that may sound. The men usually stayed sober so they could drive. Why couldn't Bob be like that? My friends' husbands *liked* their wives, even thought they were entertaining.

"People *like* me," I said. "Are you jealous that people like me so much?"

"Don't you get it?" he said. "We're in our forties. When are you going to act like it?"

I shook my head, convinced he was determined to be old, to give up on enjoying life.

"Life is for the living," I said. I said that a lot.

The truth was that I was embarrassed. I didn't like being falling-down drunk. But the only person I hurt that night was myself.

Later that summer, we went to a writers' party across town. I used to spend my time at these parties meeting people, connecting about work, enjoying other writers' stories. But at this party, I drank and smoked outside with a handful of friends.

By the time Bob came outside to say he wanted to go, I was flat-out drunk, but that didn't stop me from saying I was fine to drive, as he was even drunker than I was. I had a rule for drinking and driving. Most drunks do. If you're seeing double, you can't drive. If you can see straight without having to squint one eye closed, then you can.

Just a mile or so from the party, I saw the blue and red lights behind me. My heart dropped into my stomach.

"Shit," Bob said.

I rolled down my window for the police officer, a young man with a clean-shaven baby face. He said I had a taillight out and asked for my license and registration. I handed it over. He disappeared to his squad car. When he returned, he handed me back my paperwork.

"Your car reeks of alcohol," he said, and he had me get out.

On the sidewalk, the policeman moved his penlight side to side while I followed it with my eyes. I never broke eye contact with that light, but here's some information for all you potential drunk drivers out there: cops aren't concerned with eye contact. They're watching to see if your eyes flicker, which is what happens when you're intoxicated.

He told me to wait on the sidewalk with his partner while he ran my plates. I watched the cars slow down to gawk at this foolish middle-aged woman pulled over for drunk driving.

When he came back, he said he would let me go because there was nothing on my record, but that I had to call a cab and leave my car there. He told me I was putting other people at risk, including children.

"I'm sorry," I said, but the shame wouldn't go away. The cars still slowed to watch.

His partner, a woman, said, "You're lucky he took pity on you."

"I'm sorry," I said. *I'm sorry. I'm sorry.*

We waited for a taxi. The next day, hungover like so many other days, I rode with Bob as we drove to pick up my car.

I know people who have gotten DUIs, and I was shocked

to hear it from a few of them. They didn't drink much, but one night, they happened to have a glass or two of wine, and a cop pulled them over, and then they had to have Breathalyzers installed in their cars, and for a year, they had to blow into them before going anywhere. I was lucky. I was extraordinarily lucky, and there was no real reason why.

For the first time, I wondered: *Do I have a drinking problem?*

I tried the words out on Bob. He said, "You think?" His answer didn't surprise me, but I realized he wasn't the safest person for me to talk to about this.

I made a new rule, struck a bargain with myself: no driving after more than two glasses of wine. Three, tops.

I wanted to be better. I wanted to be better for me, and I wanted to be better for Bob so he would finally choose me, and I wanted to be better for our children. I read books about drinking, books about *women* and drinking. I reread Caroline Knapp's *Drinking: A Love Story*, which is my favorite memoir about addiction. I bought workbooks that I didn't fill out. I tried to throw myself into my writing. I tried watering down my wine, so I could drink more, and longer, without getting sloppy.

I joined a gym and went faithfully every other day, following a program in the hopes of getting my body back to what it was. Somewhere in the past year or two, I had gained twenty-five pounds. I had been the same size my entire life, moving perhaps ten pounds between a size six and a size eight. Suddenly, I noticed my clothes didn't fit. In middle age, our bodies change. We know that. Metabolism slows down. Arms spread. Middles spread. We have to work harder at the gym than we used to. But inside, somewhere, I knew that this weight gain was almost solely because of the wine.

An average glass of wine, which is five fluid ounces, has approximately 125 calories. It also has about six grams of sugar, which is more than a teaspoon of sugar per glass. And let's face it, my glasses of wine were not five ounces. If I was drinking a bottle per night, which is approximately four to five glasses of wine, then daily, I was consuming 500 to 625 calories of wine and sixteen grams of sugar. That's not even considering that late at night, I often made some questionable food choices. I figured midnight was a great time to eat half a block of cheese or to cook myself some noodles with butter and salt. I didn't need a nutrition expert to help me figure out why I had gained weight.

This bothered me a lot, even more than some of the other ways drinking was messing with my life. I *hated* how much this concerned me. Let's blame the patriarchy. Let's blame the media and the fashion industry and capitalism. They're the ones who have tied women's sense of self-worth to being thin, right?

I tried cutting out all bread and pasta. I gave up *most food* so I could keep drinking and smoking and stop gaining weight. I called it my no-grain-all-pain diet.

Women and our bodies. Will we ever escape the focus on our physical forms? Will we ever stop denying ourselves? I'm tired of caring about whether my body has bulges or cellulite or spots or spreads. I'm tired of caring about something that has no bearing on whether I will be loved or successful or a good mother. And yet I do care, because the pressure is impossible to ignore when our culture denigrates fat people, assumes skinny people are good and healthy, and believes fat people are lazy and sick. It's bullshit how people in our society make it their business to judge what others do with their bodies. Who I fuck, how many donuts I eat, how much I smoke…none of it is anyone's business but mine. This moralizing around people's bodies, especially women's, is unconscionable. It also happens to be very profitable.

The Skinny Vine company makes wines such as Slim Chardonnay and Thin Zin. Bethenny Frankel from the *Real Housewives* series started the Skinnygirl wine collection, which features a bevy of low-calorie wines. In the UK, McWilliams Wines teamed up with Weight Watchers to sell a series of low-calorie wines. Just recently, I saw a magazine in the grocery store that had the headline, "Lose thirty pounds by drinking wine!" That's hard to pass up, even when I know the only way to lose weight through drinking is to become so dependent that you drink all day and night and eat almost nothing, a phenomenon often referred to as "drunkorexia."

A thirteen-year Harvard study of twenty thousand women found that women who drank half a bottle of wine per day were at lower risk for obesity than those who didn't. The National Institute on Alcohol Abuse and Alcoholism determined that if people replaced food for wine, calorie for calorie, they tended to lose weight.* All I know is *I* got fat drinking wine.

Then there was my smoking. Smoking was, in many ways, the worse problem. Smoking and drinking were one and the same for me in that whenever I had one, I wanted the other. I joked, "I only smoke when I drink. But I drink every day." Ha ha. It would have been funnier if it weren't so true. I tried to limit my smoking to five cigarettes per night. I'd manage that for a day or two, but after just one night with friends in a backyard, I was back to ten or fifteen.

Accurate statistics about women and alcohol are hard to find. Many women carry a great deal of shame about drinking, so they minimize their self-reported answers. What we do know, however, is that in the past decade, problematic drinking among middle-aged women has increased significantly.† Men used to be more commonly arrested for drunk driving, as well as targeted more heavily for alcohol marketing. Women now have the dubious honor of leading in both areas, and women over forty have the highest arrest rate for drunk

---

* Antonia Hoyle and Tony Edwards, "How wine can help you lose weight: It defies conventional wisdom but some women insist a nightly glass of red keeps them slim and experts now say they may be right," *Daily Mail*, May 10, 2015, http://www.dailymail.co.uk/femail /article-3075931/How-wine-help-lose-weight-defies-conventional -wisdom-women-insist-nightly-glass-red-keeps-slim-experts-say -right.html.

† Steven Reinberg, "More Older Women Are Drinking Hard," CBS News, March 29, 2017, https://www.cbsnews.com/news/more-older -women-baby-boomers-binge-drinking/.

driving. Binge drinking used to be the main concern regarding alcohol abuse among both men and women, but we now see more "high functioning" alcoholism, primarily among women who drink a lot, steadily, often at home, and still manage to get their children to school, make it to work on time, and cook dinner for their families.[‡]

What has caused this increase in drinking among women in their forties? Some theories include hormonal changes, gender role ambiguity, and job and family stressors. For many women, life was simpler before mortgages and children and failed marriages. But I think something more disturbing is happening, something about how drinking has shifted from recreational socializing to full-scale addiction, something about how women have become a more despairing lot. Women are twice as likely as men to suffer from depression and anxiety, and it's hardly revelatory to say that behind most addiction is despair.[§] Or maybe it is. Maybe we talk too often about addiction as a disease that other people struggle with, people who line up outside the county shelter or sleep in their car under a bridge. Not me, and certainly not you, right?

Not all sober people are necessarily good, obviously,

[‡]   Gabrielle Glaser, *Her Best-Kept Secret: Why Women Drink—And How They Can Regain Control* (New York: Simon & Schuster, 2013), chapter 2.

[§]   This statistic can be found through many resources, but here is one: World Health Organization, "Gender and Women's Mental Health," accessed March 14, 2016, http://www.who.int/mental_health /prevention/genderwomen/en/.

and not all addicts are bad people either. They're your partner or your neighbor. They're your sister or your kid's teacher. They might be me and you.

Five

I needed a goddamn break.

EACH TIME I WALKED INTO THE HOUSE, THE MESS overwhelmed me. I didn't know how to deal with our domestic chaos. There were muddy tracks through the living room and piles of coats and backpacks and books. The kitchen cabinets were open and covered with sticky fingerprints. Dirty socks were strewn on the counter. Bacon grease coated the stove. I couldn't walk through the playroom. Crumbs were ground into the carpet. Even Bob's and my bedroom was no respite. He sometimes showered up to five times a day and used a fresh towel each time because he'd left the other towels wet and dirty and hung over the side of the bed.

He tried to clean, but he admitted he was no good at it. He would start the dishes but leave half of them in the sink, the dishwasher open. He left paper towels in the sink. He did laundry but tossed unmatched socks into random drawers around the house. I tried to finish his attempts at domesticity, but it was almost impossible to stay on top of, and in the end, nothing got done. The house was flat-out disgusting, and Bob and I blamed each other.

I also had three careers—counseling, teaching, and writing—and I couldn't leave any of my work at an office each day. I had too much to do, and there was still never enough money.

In the mornings, one of us would get the children to school. In our first year of living together, the children went to three different schools; Bob's two went to one school, Griffin went to another, and Ezra was part of a carpool that brought him thirty-five miles to a special school for autistic kids. On the mornings I drove the carpool, I was consistently ten minutes late picking up the other two kids because I had to get Griffin to school first. On the afternoons I drove the carpool, Bob was home alone with our three other kids for much of the afternoon since traffic was terrible after three. By the time I got home with Ezra—often not until five—the children were buzzing through the house. Cereal bar wrappers and empty juice boxes stuck to the couch. On the dining table were plates with half-finished peanut butter and jelly sandwiches.

In the midst of this, I would find Bob pacing somewhere, deep in thought about a new business scheme, lost in his thoughts the way my father had been when I was growing up. Meanwhile, the children tormented each other, watched too much television, made messes, and rarely cleaned up after themselves, no matter how often we reminded them.

Sometimes after school, Bob tried to organize activities for the children. Most could not include all the children, largely because Ezra wouldn't do well wherever Bob planned to go, or I couldn't figure out how to give all the children the attention they'd need while keeping Ezra from wandering off. I did not fancy, for example, community pools, which was one of Bob's go-to activities for his children. I loved fenced-in parks. I loved anywhere I was not in a constant panic one of the children might disappear or die. I loved anywhere I didn't have to worry about Ezra inappropriately approaching strangers, saying bizarre things to them, and then, perhaps, taking off with one of their children's toys.

Life at home was stressful. I tried to hide my feelings from Bob, but I sometimes looked for excuses to get away from it. I wanted to be alone with my boys. Sometimes it felt like if I could just have that, if I could have a day or two with only their energy, which was familiar and so different from the rest of the household, I might be able to see things clearly. I might be able to have the clarity I needed to make the changes I knew I had to make.

One summer when Bob and I were three years deep into the misery of our relationship, I took my boys to visit my father and his wife at their vacation home in Massachusetts. Ezra was ten, and Griffin was seven. They were both easy to travel with. As long as Ezra had his iPad and his brother, he was happy. In fact, no one I know is happier than Ezra. While Griffin and I are notorious complainers, Ezra doesn't complain about anything. He asks lots of questions. He wants to know what's coming, and he wants to know why, but if he gets answers, he's good. Ezra is more easygoing than Griffin. Michael and I joke that Griffin is really the one with special needs, because even as a newborn, he seemed riddled with existential angst. He'd get a poopy diaper, and his cries were so intense, as if he were shaking a fist at the sky, thinking, *Why, God, why?*

My sister and brother-in-law came from San Francisco with their daughter, and the younger kids rode scooters around the cul-de-sac. The next day, they wanted to go to the park, but Ezra didn't want to go anywhere. This is typical of him, especially if he's in unfamiliar surroundings. He prefers what he already knows, so he won't get surprised by something novel, something he won't know how to handle. He prefers Wi-Fi and his iPad. My dad, his wife, and my sister's family took Griffin with them to the park while I stayed at the house with Ezra. I read. I walked from room to room. I looked at photos of the grandchildren, stood on the back deck, watched the birds light from tree to tree. There was nothing else to do, really, so I found a bottle of red wine, grabbed a glass and my smokes, and sat on the deck. In the couple of hours they were gone, I made it three-quarters of the way through the bottle and smoked maybe half a dozen cigarettes. By now, it was habit. This was how I got away from my feelings.

When everyone came back, my dad said, "What are you doing?"

I said, "What does it look like?"

He said nothing, but he frowned.

The next day, everyone wanted to go into Northampton, a town I'd once frequented and still loved. I wanted to go. It would be my one chance, since I now lived so far away. My niece was going to get her ears pierced, and then they were planning to walk around and get the kids ice cream. Ezra wouldn't go. I tried to convince him, but I knew he'd spend the whole time saying, "I want to go home." It would be miserable for both him and us.

I said, "Can someone stay here with Ezra?"

My sister and brother-in-law couldn't stay because they wanted to be with their daughter when she got her ears pierced. And my father said he wouldn't ask his wife to stay because he knew she wanted to go too.

They left, and I stayed with Ezra. I hadn't left the property since we'd arrived. We'd traveled all this way, and I couldn't help but feel alone, not just in the house but in my life. I love Ezra more than anything. He is my light, my heart, my soul. But I would have liked a break. Just a small one. Sometimes it felt like there was no one with me but my grief. A palpable thing, always riding with me since Ezra had been born. My father couldn't see that. He didn't want to see it, and he never had.

Stuck in that house, I couldn't take a walk or write or even do yoga because I was too upset. But I could drink.

I went through two bottles in the five hours they were gone. I read. I smoked. I talked to a friend on the phone.

When they returned, my dad looked at the empty bottles. "Put bottles in the recycling," he said.

"I'm not here to make your life difficult," I said, angry and riled up from the wine. Why was I here at all? It felt like there was nowhere for me to be, nowhere that would hold me.

"Maybe not, but you're drinking a lot of wine."

I shook my head. "What else should I do, Dad?" I said. "I've been here alone with Ezra for three days straight!" I stomped off to my room like a child. I hate how I always feel this way around my parents, like I never grew up.

Later that evening, the Wi-Fi went out for a few minutes, and Ezra screamed and cried. "What's wrong with the internet?" he yelled between sobs.

"Jesus," my dad said. "Calm down, Ez. It's not such a big deal."

I wanted to hit him. I wanted to scream. I wanted to drink every last drop of wine in his house. He had no idea who Ezra was, who I was, what our lives were. My father has his good qualities, but his inability to put his family over his own needs, or his need to keep his wife happy, had taken its toll over the years.

The Wi-Fi started working again, but by then, I couldn't stop the tears that sometimes came like that, suddenly and overpowering. My father didn't notice, or he tried not to notice, and I didn't want him to see anyway. I didn't like to be vulnerable around my parents, but especially my father, because it was inevitably a reminder of how I felt they didn't care all that much. So familiar, that old pain. And with these emotions, I felt like a teenager, like a big, whiny baby. *Daddy doesn't love me!* Please. I hated myself right then. I hated my life. I hated everything.

I escaped outside with the glass of wine and pack of cigarettes. My brother-in-law came outside and joined me after a bit.

"How's it going?" he asked.

"Just fine," I said. We looked at each other. I smiled as best I could. My brother-in-law is a good man, and checking on me, keeping me company after witnessing what had just happened between my father and me? I loved him for that.

The next day, driving us to the airport, my father glanced at me and said, "You know, there's a lot of sugar in wine. That's probably how you gained that weight."

After that visit, I didn't speak to my father much. Having him see something so true and problematic about me brought tremendous shame. He had taught me to pretend nothing was wrong, so for him to call out the way I wasn't okay made me want to run even further away.

Drinking felt like running away, but what I was doing was keeping my problems closer, more alive. I made them big, surely bigger than they needed to be. I'd text a friend about one of Bob's indiscretions, like those condoms. Or I'd call a friend and say, "I need to come over right now." And we'd drink while we analyzed the implications, the possible recourses. By the time I saw Bob, I'd be drunk and riled up and ready to leave him.

One night, a few girlfriends and I were at Julia's. We were in the kitchen, and somehow we ended up comparing our breasts. *Somehow* seems dishonest. Wine was obviously part of the equation that night. Each of us held our shirts up under our chins and unhooked our bras while the rest of us assessed. One of us had a smaller set that was flat on top from breastfeeding. The next was a perfect size C. Okay, maybe mine weren't perfect, but just stay with the story. The other two had beautiful, bulbous size Ds, both seemingly untouched by breastfeeding. The point is, these were all lovely sets of boobs. And we were proud. In our forties, postnursing, past when we women are supposed to be proud of our boobs, we *were* proud. But there was no question that Julia's were the loveliest.

Julia's husband, Mitch, was the only man there, and he was outside stoking the fire pit. We went back out, shared our conclusion, and he wholeheartedly agreed that his wife had the most beautiful breasts in all the land. Not thinking much of it, I wrote a quick post on Facebook about our competition. When I got home, Bob was pissed at me.

"That's sick!" he said. "Why do you need other people to think about your breasts?"

"You're missing the point," I said. "We were having fun. A bunch of fortysomething women comparing our boobs? It was *funny*."

"It's not funny!" he said, and he took a pillow to sleep on the couch.

There were so many times like this when I wondered, *Am I insane? Is what I did that terrible? Did I deserve that kind of response from Bob?* Later, I told one of my boob-comparing friends about Bob's response and she said, "Jesus, it's not like we were fingering each other. It's not like we were having some sort of bacchanalian orgy."

Bob's anger had more to do with my drinking than anything else, really. By then, I was drinking around my kids. They needed me, but I was too busy obsessing over my pain. I would get my kids to bed, slurring as I read them a story, and the whole time, I couldn't wait to get back outside where I could drink and smoke and obsess some more about my relationship with Bob.

When I was drunk, I was caught up in my own perspective and had no room for anyone else's. I had more of a relationship with wine than with Bob. Drinking, like any addiction, kept me inside the fantasy I had that I was unlovable, that I was garbage, that I would always, always live inside this despair. It also kept me from seeing my own contribution to what was wrong with us. It would be years before I understood that I was creating as many problems between Bob and me through my intense romance with my pain as he was through his issues with commitment.

Somewhere around this time, I started going to a therapist. I'd been in and out of therapy since I was nineteen. This time, though, I went with a clear agenda.

I needed to figure out how to get out of this relationship.

My therapist, Lucy, listened to me as I spoke about Bob, about my sense of myself as a consolation prize, about my past with my mother, about my friends.

She asked, "How much do you drink?"

"Oh, you know, just socially," I said.

"But how much?"

"You know, two or three glasses of wine."

"How often?"

"Just with friends," I said. "Just after five o'clock. Just for fun."

We discussed the fact that I'd never been a drinker before. We discussed what I got out of drinking. Before going into private practice, she'd worked as a substance abuse counselor, and she believed that alcoholism was always a progressive disease that demanded abstinence.

"I might have a drinking problem," I said.

"You might," she said.

But I didn't believe that yet, because I looked around and saw so many other women my age doing the same thing.

Drinking among middle-aged women has become a *thing* in our culture. Girls' night out, and liquid-based book clubs, and those *Real Housewives* episodes where they drink out of huge wineglasses and trash talk whoever isn't there. Add children, and there are blogs, websites, and Facebook groups named shit like "Moms Who Drink and Swear" and "OMG I So Need a Glass of Wine or I'm Gonna Sell My Kids." There's wine in sippy cups and wine at moms' groups and wine for the grown-ups at kids' parties. T-shirts for women sport slogans like *Guns n' Rosé*, *My favorite workout is wine*, *Half full* (with a picture of a half-full wineglass), *Therapy* (with a wineglass as the Y), *I tried running but I kept spilling my wine*, *A day without wine isn't over yet*, and so many more.

I guess it's funny to need a drink when you're a woman!

It's become a lifestyle, a way to take back something we never got to have. We get to have it all now! And thanks to having it all, we're exhausted. *How else are we supposed to get through this?* we ask, finally getting to say the truth. Kids are hard. Life is hard. Everything is so damn *hard*.

I saw two women having lunch at a restaurant the other day. They split a salad. *They split a salad!* But they each had their own glasses of chardonnay, and as the hour passed, they each had their own bottle. Women aren't supposed to eat in public; it's unseemly. We already knew that. So, by God, let us drink.

A place called PlayDate PDX opened in the Pearl District, a part of northwest Portland that was once warehouses, nondescript storefronts, and a few artsy loft buildings. Now, it's filled with expensive condos and high-end boutiques, so PlayDate PDX fits right in. It was a large, restaurant-style room, painstakingly hip with bistro tables and chairs, a few leather couches, large flat-screen televisions, and a gigantic, multilevel play structure at one end. They offered a full menu of overpriced food—and wine and beer. A friend once said about PlayDate PDX, "Screaming children, frazzled parents, and alcohol. What could go wrong?" You might be surprised to hear that, for us at least, very little went wrong. There were a few scrapes and bruises, some hurt feelings, and some people confused by Ezra's odd behavior. Beyond that, the only drawback was how expensive the food was and how much the children always seemed to want to eat. The wine wasn't cheap either, but that didn't stop me. By the time we left that place, I was practically twitching from nerve damage, and my checking account was about one hundred dollars lighter, but I usually had a decent enough buzz to get me through.

We women need our wine. Don't judge us. It's not heroin. It's not cocaine. It's just wine! Women's magazines tell us it's good for us. The CDC even says so! It has antioxidants and potassium. What's more, stress will hurt you and everyone around you faster than wine will. If, that is, you drink just one or two glasses a night.

My days of stopping after one or two (or three) glasses were way behind me.

Six

I was something resembling happy.

Bob may have had legitimate concerns about my drinking, particularly after my near-miss with Portland's finest, but I had my own worries—namely, his ongoing desire to stick his dick into women other than me.

When the person you're with says he wants to sleep with other women, you might begin to snoop. You might snoop when given the opportunity—such as when he leaves his phone at home by mistake, or when he doesn't password protect his computer, or when he does but you know his passwords. And when you snoop, you will probably find something that will upset you. It had become another cycle with Bob and me. When he grew distant, I went through his stuff. I once found a list of pros and cons about me. I found a task list that included

"Decide on Kerry." I found so much proof that he couldn't love me, which always seemed like a good reason to drink.

People who snoop are usually in pain, and they often look for something to make another person responsible for that pain. One of my clients had a partner who constantly snooped. She said, "Facts will not lead to trust." She was right. Trust is something you have when you are a solid person who knows how to love, who believes you are lovable.

I was not that person yet.

One afternoon when Bob was out, I snooped through his email. He said he'd told me everything about his struggle with needing to pursue other women, but he hadn't. There was more! This was just one more thing, but it was a pretty hefty thing. In an email to his ex-wife, he told her he had never stopped being in love with her, and he added that he felt this way even though being with me was good for his career. *I was good for his career.*

My very first thought: How much wine is in my house?

I went to Lauren's house, where I knew there would be wine and cigarettes. We drank and smoked while I cried.

"How much longer?" she asked me. "How much longer will you do this with him?"

This was it, I said. The final straw. I was done with him!

I called two other friends, and they came over. They were all my friends, and I loved them, but I used them that day. I used them to drink with, to sit and listen to me vent so I could stay in that sick, wild romance I was in with my pain. And this time, this email he'd written, it was so much worse than anything he'd done before, so to have my friends bear witness to it was that much more horrendous.

When Bob returned from his hike, he texted and called me, trying to understand what had happened. I wouldn't answer, so he left voicemails. "Kerry," he said, "please don't do this. Be reasonable." He grew angry and desperate and threatened to throw my things into the yard. It was all very messy, and having my friends witness his behavior was even worse than the email. But I was drunk, and the wine eventually carried away any ounce of reason I might have had and left me in a sea of lovely nothingness.

That night, I stayed at Lauren's house. I lay in the guest bed, drunk and sad, hurt beyond repair, unable to move forward. I stared at the spinning ceiling, praying for a way to feel better, for guidance. It didn't occur to me that one obvious solution was to stop drinking. No one can see anything clearly in a haze of booze and confusion.

When I went home the next day, Bob and I sat across from each other at the dining room table. We were both exhausted and tired of all the fighting. And I had a brutal hangover to boot.

Bob said, "I think we need to break up."

My heart dropped under my chest. I stopped breathing. I had been at my friend's house saying the same thing, but sitting there now, with *him* saying it, I wanted to die. I didn't really want our relationship to end. As a drunk, I thought I had control over all this. I thought I was running the show. Many drunks do. I drank to feel more in control of my feelings, but while I was slinging back those drinks, the world slipped into a tornado around me and picked up everything I cared about. I was beginning to realize that maybe it wasn't just Bob ruining us.

For the next few days, we went through the motions of life. The kids were coming back to us in a day. We decided not to say anything to them yet. We had a trip planned for later in the month, a writing retreat we'd set up in the Olympic Mountains. That would be our last time together as a couple, we decided. Bob started looking at apartments. Every second of every day felt like a chore. I waited for the hour when I could drink again, which had, at one point, been 5:00 but had changed over time to 4:00. Now, I waited and watched the clock: 2:00…3:00…3:30. I started drinking earlier just to get through.

My friends tried to cheer me up. Julia said, "Let's go to Vegas, just us." I said I wanted to be in a coma for a few months until I was through the worst pain, and Lauren said, "You need a Mexicoma," a reference to the first *Sex and the City* movie, when Carrie and her friends went to Mexico after Mr. Big left her at the altar. I knew my friends had my back, and they knew how to make me laugh. But I was still inconsolable.

At night, Bob and I talked about what was happening to us, and we drank. I didn't feel angry. I had never been an angry drunk. Besides, it didn't make sense to me to be angry at people for not loving me.

Bob and I got to the Olympic Mountain retreat in early evening. I grabbed a bottle of wine and my smokes and went out onto the deck. Bob frowned. But what did it matter? We were breaking up, and I didn't give a shit anymore whether he judged me. In hindsight, maybe he wasn't judging me. Maybe he just wanted to be together this one last time, without wine and cigarettes between us.

Outside, the sky was clear, stars pricking the darkness. Here in the country, I could see the Milky Way, its soft stretch. Moths and gnats swirled around the light. I tried to envision my life going forward, but the pit in my stomach was like an endless cavern. The wine couldn't touch it.

We fucked that night and the next morning and throughout the day. We fucked ourselves into each other. We fucked at our sorrow. During the day, we sat at our computers and wrote. It was the third day, I believe, when Bob had what he called a "revelation."

We were visiting a lodge near the house where we were staying so we could use their Wi-Fi, and a man and woman were there with their teenage grandson. I struck up a conversation with them when their grandson went to the bathroom, because I was touched that he was here in the middle of nowhere with his grandparents rather than doing all the things teenagers would usually rather do. They told us their story. Their son had died in a car crash. The boy's mother had left long ago. Every year, around Mother's Day, they take their grandson, whom they care for like their own son, on a trip. She said, "Mother's Day is a sad time for us. So we get away to a place like this where we can look at a lake and think about nothing and just be together."

It was right after this conversation that Bob said, "Take a walk with me."

We went on a short hike that ended at a waterfall. All

around us were dripping ferns and old growth and moss. Green. Tons and tons of green. Bob described his thoughts, that he'd been preventing happiness because of his divorce, that he didn't want to be without me, that he understood something he hadn't before. I loved him, and he had been pushing away my love. I was a drunk, but he drank too. He was limited too. He cried. He had never done that before with me. He cried as he told me. He cried when we drove back to the house. He cried as he opened the gate to the property.

When we were in the house, he asked me, again, to marry him. Again, I said yes.

We celebrated with a bottle of wine. We drank out of happiness. We drank out of fear. We drank out of disbelief. There was always a good reason to drink.

The next morning, he told me he'd stayed up all night, just watching me sleep.

I found out much later, long after it was too late, that he had slept with another woman just a week earlier. He decided he was ready to commit to me because he'd finally gotten his dick wet with someone other than me, and he thought it was out of his system.

Should I have seen that coming? Perhaps when I learned about this infidelity, I shouldn't have been so surprised. When I was enmeshed in my relationship with Bob, a friend told me, "He's going to cheat. That is inevitable." Of course! Of course it was! But drinking kept me from looking too hard and from dealing with what I saw, and then seeing the things I did see made me drink some more.

This is what I mean about stories. There are the ones we think are real, and the ones we thought were in place, and the ones someone else will tell. Somewhere inside all these stories is the truth about how my drinking became a problem even as I used it to avoid dealing with all the other problems.

I didn't believe I was an alcoholic (which is a layman's term for alcohol dependence). I have a friend who's in AA, and she laughed when I told her I'd started watering down my wine so I could keep drinking without getting drunk. "What the hell kind of alcoholic doesn't want to be drunk?" she said. On the other hand, some friends thought I *abused* alcohol. I can't argue with that now, because at my lowest point, I would want to drink from almost the moment I woke up, and once I started, I rarely wanted to stop.

But how do we differentiate between alcoholism (alcohol dependence) and alcohol abuse (problem drinking)? These are different only in that recovery from alcohol dependence demands abstinence, while alcohol abusers may be able to establish a controlled relationship to alcohol. What abusers have is a habit. That sounds so much nicer, doesn't it? *I'm not an addict; I have a bad habit!* And in fact, some researchers argue that alcohol dependence isn't a disease but that alcohol use is a learned habit that can be unlearned over time.* While there is no simple test to determine whether

---

* Herbert Fingarette, *Heavy Drinking: The Myth of Alcoholism as a Disease* (Berkeley: University of California Press, 1988), and Marc Lewis, *The Biology of Desire: Why Addiction is Not a Disease* (New York: PublicAffairs, 2015).

you have a drinking problem or are a problem drinker, these studies suggest that problem drinkers might be able to moderate—eventually.

Moderating wasn't on my radar yet, because my problem drinking, or whatever it was, didn't seem nearly as big a problem as, well, my life.

Getting married was stupid. We did it because we didn't know how else to stay together. I know it sounds dumb. I was a middle-aged woman with two kids and three jobs. My specialty as a therapist was sex and relationships! You'd think I would make better choices, but I was making bad choices left and right. This marriage was so different from my first. My marriage to Michael had started out almost magical—hopeful, full of possibility and happiness—but this time around, marriage was about Bob's and my desperation to create solidity where there was none. This time, our children begged us to do it. (Griffin denies this. He says, "I didn't even *like* Bob. Why would I want you to *marry* him?") Bob and I were both so damaged by then, we were like two funeral directors resigned to planning our own funerals.

There was little joy in the planning. My father wasn't interested in hearing about our wedding plans, and he certainly wasn't interested in paying for it. How could I even suggest he should be part of this travesty my life had become? The worst part was that I agreed with him. My life was a mess, something I had never anticipated. I wanted to be married again, to have a husband. I was in love with Bob, even if that love had become horribly tainted by our addiction to each other. I knew, in that way we all sometimes feel in our guts, that I was making a terrible mistake.

Bob's family didn't want much to do with us either, and they openly objected to our engagement. They questioned his intentions and mine. Everyone in his family had come to his first wedding—all eight of them—but this time, their RSVPs slowly came back: No. No. No. His father and just one of his brothers would show up for our wedding. No one wanted to accept it as something real.

My mother was skeptical too. When Michael and I were still married, she and her husband had always included him in their plans for my visits, often offering to pay for his ticket. They'd never liked Bob much, and now that we were engaged, they barely even acknowledged him. Sometimes they asked in tight voices, "And how is Bob doing?" But they didn't tell me to say hello or send their love. They didn't send presents or cards for my soon-to-be stepchildren's birthdays.

When no one wants to recognize your marriage, it's difficult to believe in yourself, to believe you've done the right thing, that you've made a choice that resonates with anyone other than you. Bob and I knew we were on our own, that this was up to us and only us.

Everything about being middle-aged, about failure, came to light. I tried not to think too much about my first wedding. Michael and I were engaged for a year and a half, and that is still one of the happiest times of my life. I surprised myself by getting excited and involved in the planning. Michael and I had no children then, no autism, no financial failures, no reason to believe anything bad would come. The hopefulness of that part of my life still makes my throat tight. All I wanted was to feel that hopefulness again, that belief in the possibilities to come. But I didn't feel anything like that. I knew there was not much to be hopeful about when it came to Bob's and my relationship. I knew that my career would not suddenly take off again. I wasn't dreaming about an exciting future. I don't know if it's middle age or the fact that it was a second marriage, but the whole thing had a film of meh over it. And drinking numbed my negativity just enough to keep me moving ahead with our plans.

The night I stayed over at Lauren's marked the beginning of a shift in our friendship. I was embarrassed that I kept moving forward with Bob. She was fed up with the stories she'd heard about him, and not just because of his behavior with me. He actively disliked some of my friends, and he wasn't shy about letting them know. Gradually, he had made it clear there were certain girlfriends of mine he didn't want in our house. He argued with me often about some of their behavior, their drinking, things they said that he misunderstood to be mean or offensive. His desire to isolate me from some friends might have been alarming if I weren't caught up in the addictiveness of our relationship and my drinking. It seemed natural to choose my soon-to-be husband over a girlfriend, but in hindsight, his anger toward them was extreme. My friends hadn't done anything to hurt him or our relationship. Bob and I were doing that to ourselves.

There's something that happens when you drink too

much and too often with friends. Small issues become gigantic. A single story gets taken apart and chewed to bits until you are certain everything is fucked and awful and insane. And there's no way to change anyone's mind later. This is what happened with Lauren. The day I found that thing when I'd snooped, we sat around drinking and smoking and steaming, building a fire so big about Bob that, when it came to her, I would never be able to put it out.

She was sick of watching me lose myself in Bob's and my relationship. She was tired of worrying about me, although I couldn't have articulated that then. At the time, it felt like she couldn't support me, and that was all. We can't know what's inside other people's hearts. And we can't know what's right for other people wherever they are in their lives either. Many of my friends have said to me, "You deserve someone like I have." Maybe they didn't say those exact words, but that's what I heard. I would never want what they have. I only want what my heart wants, and my heart wants what it wants because it is hell-bent on becoming whole.

This is part of my drinking story too.

My heart wants to be whole. And drinking was a panacea for the ways in which it wasn't.

Lauren's friendship wasn't the only casualty of my drinking and this disaster that was my relationship with Bob. I lost friends because of the ways drinking blows everything up into a shitstorm, into a firework display of feelings. And suddenly something that was hurtful becomes the most horrible thing that ever could have happened.

We held a reception in the place we first met, a house Naomi and her husband had bought and converted into a space for writers to work. I rented a tent for the lawn, with wooden folding chairs and white tablecloths laid over picnic tables and a hodgepodge of vintage plates, glasses, and silver. Bud vases with bundles of white and pale-green flowers stretched across each table, along with tea lights. Inside was the bar and karaoke. I wore an antique, tea-colored dress with a pale-pink sash. I bought Bob's daughter a dress to match mine, and Bob and our three boys wore gingham shirts, bow ties, and delicate boutonnieres.

I devoted a healthy chunk of the money we put toward the wedding to wine and beer. We'd gotten married at city hall the week before, so we had no ceremony. We focused on having fun, and the night went off without a hitch. Even the kids were happy, running around the property together (it was fenced in!). Everything was great—until my father made an unexpected toast.

He stood up and said a few things about being happy to be there. He said the food was great. And then he said, "I don't really understand why they're doing this." I felt everyone stop breathing, and I didn't dare look at Bob. After he finished, my father walked over to me and said, "Was that okay?"

"Oh yeah, thanks," I said. "That was great, Dad."

Then, for three straight months, I was something resembling happy. There was some peace between Bob and me. We kissed each other hello when returning home. We had family dinners when the kids were with us. We did all the things a married couple should do.

But getting married hadn't changed much of anything. I felt as if I'd been in one of two situations for so long: I was either desperate about Bob—*he doesn't love me, he wants to get away, he is considering not being with me*—or I fantasized about leaving him. Now, married for just a few months, I still had these same misgivings.

My whole life had been like this, of course. My father was unavailable. My mother, even gone from my life, suffocated me with her needs. Intimacy, or what I knew of it, was a push and pull between these two extremes. Chasing or withdrawing. Too much or too little. At this point, I knew that this was the case. I knew these thoughts were likely my monkey mind, working as it always did to prevent genuine intimacy. But awareness and action are two very different things.

I had not stopped drinking, which felt like a sign that things weren't magically perfect just because we were married. Our lives fell back into old ruts. The household was still unmanageable. I still spent much of my time outside with a glass of wine in one hand and a cigarette in the other, so familiar and comfortable. And Bob couldn't stop ruminating about other women. We couldn't seem to acknowledge that both of us had spent most of our relationship trying to get out of it, and we were both still trying to escape.

Seven

I failed at everything but sleeping.

WHILE YOU'RE DRINKING, EVERYTHING FEELS FINE. YOU STAY up, and you keep going, because you know that when it's over, when you finally set your glass in the sink, when you finally stub out that last cigarette, you'll lie in bed and think, well, fuck, here it comes. Real life. And you'll wish you could rewind to a few hours earlier. And the next day, sure as shit, there it is. *Real life.* Your alarm goes off because you must get your kids to school. You gulp down water. You take ibuprofen. You drink whatever coffee you can get down. And you wait for four o'clock, when you can get some hair of the dog and feel better again. All those daily struggles—the dishes and the kids needing dinner and the laundry and the overgrown garden and your failing career and your husband who doesn't give you enough attention and your life not at all how you pictured it—those struggles will all go away at four o'clock.

Most days, I slept in because I had to, because I had overdone it the night before. On those mornings, I knew what to expect: I would spend most of the day thinking about wine. Red wine. Thick and deep and dark enough to wash over my insides and make parts of me disappear. Make me feel like things were okay after all, even when they weren't. I watched the clock. Noon. Three. Still too early. Four. Four thirty. Then finally, five o'clock would come. Wine o'clock, that old joke. Except it wasn't all that funny, because I was struggling with this wine thing. My friends were too. We talked about it regularly. We said, *I must stop. I did something stupid again. Really. Need to just have one or two glasses a day, just a few times a week.*

I managed to get my kids off to school with breakfast in their bellies and to show up at my office, most days, to greet my therapy clients. I need to acknowledge that I did not show up to therapy sessions drunk or even tipsy. I always waited until I was done with work to start drinking. I did worry about what my clients might find out. If a client mentioned she went to a bar, I'd wait until she was done, and then ask, "Which bar?" I'd tick that bar off my list of possible hangouts.

There's a sequence many problem drinkers go through. They set rules. It's okay to drink, as long as I never drink alone. It's okay to drink, as long as I only drink at night. It's okay to day drink, as long as it's only on weekends. Okay, or if someone else is drinking with me. Or, okay, if it's after noon.

To this day, I read other people's accounts of their alcoholism and I think, "Well, I never kept fifths of vodka in my car and snuck sips before picking up my kids from school. I don't have to drink every last drop of alcohol in the house until it's gone. I don't drink liquor just because it's the only alcohol in the house." So I can't be *that* bad off. I can't have a *real* drinking problem. But here's the deal: once you start wondering if you have a drinking problem, once you start checking your stories against other people's drinking stories, you probably do have a problem.

Most nights around seven, I went inside to make sure the children were fed. I was not much for cooking—another thing Bob and I argued about—but *you* try feeding four children who all like different things, one with allergies, and then Ezra who ate almost nothing. There were just a few things they agreed to eat: tacos, spaghetti and meatballs, and chicken pot pie, so I made the same meals over and over. Then I was back outside for more smoking and drinking until nine when I went back in to get them to bed.

Usually. There were times I allowed the hours to pass and let them stay up as late as they wanted. Bob and I argued about that too. Often, it wasn't until eleven or midnight that I stood, unsteady and swerving, and made my way to my bedroom. Bob was usually already in bed, but he was a light sleeper, and drunk people are not the quietest bed companions, so he would roll over, as if letting me know without words how sick of this he was. I flossed, brushed my teeth, and washed my face, the careful behaviors of someone who refused to believe she was

Lush

79

out of control, and I got under the covers. Occasionally, Bob would drape a hand on my hip or an arm around my shoulders, but that happened less and less.

When I slept, I slept deeply, the sleep of the almost dead. It was not dreamless, but it was heavy and as foggy as Oregon's winter forests. Sleep was the best. Sleep was when I did nothing wrong, disappointed no one, and had no responsibilities to shirk. I woke miserable, wanting only more sleep. I dragged myself through the day until I was back on that stoop or in my garage. I was not quite living, and yet I thought for sure I was alive, man. I was having *fun*. I laughed a lot. I accomplished what I needed to accomplish for work.

Sometime after Bob and I married, I added a new addiction to my cocktail of wine and cigarettes: TV shows. After the children had gone to bed or as soon as the work day was over on nights the kids weren't with us, I watched episode after episode of my new favorite series. First, it was *It's Always Sunny in Philadelphia*. Then *Sons of Anarchy* alternated with *Parks and Recreation*. Next it was *Scandal*. The problem here was that by adding another piece to my addictive behaviors, I was conditioning myself to want to drink and smoke while watching TV. In other words, one initial step in quitting drinking is to replace one addiction with another, less harmful addiction. By drinking and smoking and watching TV together, I was ruling out TV as something I could do when I possibly eventually quit. Although Bob had stopped having hope, I *was* still planning to eventually change my ways.

I had obviously graduated to drinking alone. I probably

drank a bottle of wine each night, sometimes more. And I smoked when I drank, maybe fifteen cigarettes.

When I was in my thirties, focused on establishing my career and still nursing my babies, I met a couple who asked me, "Do you think it's a problem that we share a bottle of wine every night with our dinner? Does that seem excessive?"

It did seem excessive, but what did I know back then? I never drank anything.

Now that I *was* a drinker, half a bottle a night with dinner seemed perfectly okay. In fact, if I could drink just half a bottle of wine, I would call that restraint and chalk it up as a win.

When I picked up my kids from school, I saw the other mothers, those alien creatures whom I feared lived so unlike I did, whom I was certain weren't miserable like I was. We smiled politely at one another. They came straight from the gym, or else they dressed up for this "event" of picking up children. They felt a million miles away, or maybe I wanted them to be a million miles away. I didn't want what I assumed their lives were. I didn't want this—my status as a mother and wife—to be all there was to look forward to each day. My identity has always been about my work, particularly as a writer. I adore my children. I could not live on a planet that didn't have them on it too, but my purpose was and is created by my work.

My writing, however, was not doing well. My agent shook his head at most things I sent him, and when he tried to sell things of mine he believed were worthwhile, editors responded that they weren't as groundbreaking as *Loose Girl*, so they didn't want them. I felt like I was failing in almost all my roles—mother, partner, writer. Nothing held solace for me.

At school, I located my children, took them home, fed them snacks. Sometimes I went back to my office to see more clients. On my way home, I stopped at the convenience store to buy my supplies for the night. Pulling into my driveway, that brown bag next to me on the passenger seat, was like a long sigh, the best part of the day. At least it was another thing at which I wasn't failing.

My addictions have taken many forms, and all can be framed as my attempts to feel alive. When I was married to Michael, I wanted babies. I was determined to have babies. That would help me. And a house, and a renovation, and a new house after that. My friend Julia and I are still dumb enough to think a new baby would fill that hole. We say, "You have a baby. We'll share it." "No, you do it." Because we both already have two babies each, and we learned the hard way that babies fill nothing but your heart and your time. Besides, we're both in our forties. We're too tired for babies. But Julia is unrelenting. She got a puppy. That puppy is the biggest pain in her ass. Now, it's a dog and still a pain in her ass. Then she got a kitten. He's a total pain in her ass. Once, I borrowed the kitten when I was alone, Bob out of town and the children at their father's, and after a day and a half, I texted her: I'm done with the kitten. What a pain in the ass that guy was. The other day, Julia said, "I just want to live in a house without children or animals," and I laughed, because then she'd have more babies and adopt more animals, and she'd be in the same place. Sometimes it appears almost everything we do is a kind of addiction, a way to believe that maybe we can feel better than we do right now.

I went with Julia and her husband and another couple with an autistic child to a beach house with all our children for a weekend. I arrived just as Julia's autistic son was being taken home, back to Grandma's, because he had been too impossible at the beach house.

"I don't know why I make this mistake every time," Julia said as we settled on the deck with our wineglasses. "Every time, I think it will be fun for him, and instead, he throws fits because he can't, you know, walk into the ocean where he'll promptly drown."

We laughed. We took sips of our wine. I lit up a cigarette. A couple of the children were screaming inside, running up and down the stairs. Julia told me how earlier Dan, one of the other parents, had taken a basket of decorative rocks out of her son's hands just as he was about to start throwing them at the picture windows that looked out over the ocean.

"Oh my God, Julia," I said.

She shook her head. "I had to send him home."

Later, Julia's husband, Mitch, and our friend Emily took the rest of the kids to the beach. Mitch said to Emily, "I'll take the typicals. You take the specials." It was a relief watching them walk away from us, leaving the house silent and still. Later, all the kids were plugged into some sort of media, and we adults went out to the hot tub with our drinks. After, we ate dinner and drank more wine.

Sometime around midnight, Julia started to cry. I don't remember what happened in the minutes before. I'm sure that, two seconds earlier, we had been laughing our heads off about something. But here we were, Julia on the floor, the strength of her grief so large that she couldn't move. *I can't do it anymore, I can't, I can't.* Her husband, looking helpless, stood nearby, while I sat on the floor, holding and rocking her.

Later that night, after we had all finally gotten to sleep, I heard Griffin run to the bathroom to vomit. I got up to help him, clean him up, and get him back to bed. Just two hours later, Ezra woke me up with his restlessness, and I kicked him out of bed but couldn't fall back asleep. When we were all awake a few hours later, we sat bleary-eyed around the breakfast table. None of us had gotten much sleep. All of us were hungover.

The guest book for the beach house sat on the table, and I flipped through it. We joked about how we could write about our stay in which one child almost threw rocks through the windows, another puked, and one of the parents had a temporary breakdown. On one of the pages, someone had written, "Thank you for the relaxing getaway! I'm twenty-two weeks pregnant, so this was the perfect way for my husband and I to get away from life's stresses." I took the cap off the marker and wrote "JUST YOU WAIT" across the bottom of the page.

I sometimes get texts from Julia at three in the afternoon telling me she's started drinking. Her older child is not only autistic. He has a seizure disorder and mild cerebral palsy. He often trips and falls, breaking bones. Julia and Mitch have been to the emergency room more times than they've been out to dinner since their children were born. If Julia doesn't get her ass out of bed when her eleven-year-old son does, she will come downstairs to find he poured syrup all over the kitchen floor and is watching the dog lick it up. Or a phone will be fried in the microwave. Or he will have squirted catsup all over the couch.

She and I talked at times about slowing down the drinking, and she said, "Please tell me what I will get from being sober." She has tried antidepressants, marijuana, herbal remedies, exercise, as many vacations as she can afford. Nothing dulls the stress, the grief, of her life. And there I was, of no help to her. I wasn't going to help with the drinking when I couldn't do the same for myself. Julia and I were in this mess together. A lot of my friends were. And none of us could really help each other, as much as we wanted to.

Nothing about this is unique or even especially interesting. I'm not a heroin addict who stole from my grandparents. My friends never killed anyone. No one died or almost died. I never went to jail or hid bottles of gin in the back of my closet. I'm not Cat Marnell or some other interesting drug addict who is "Fucked Up and Fascinating" according to the cool hunters at Jezebel. I don't have an eating disorder or borderline person-ality disorder. I'm not even young. I'm just some middle-aged woman who finds life to be trying.

Life continues. You'll have to clean up your kids' barf again. The water heater will need to be replaced. Your car will break down. Someone will stop paying child support. When would it be safe to stop drinking? Would things ever feel less hard? What would I do instead to soften the edges? This spot in an addict's life feels like the hardest hurdle. In the stages of change model, it's called "contemplation."* You contemplate changing. You weigh the pros and cons. You start imagining a life without drinking. For me, so much of it was wondering if stopping was worth it.

One of my clients, a sex addict, continues to cheat on his wife. When I ask him why he stays with her, he says because she loves him. He knows each time he's about to cheat, and he tells himself not to every time, but the voice saying not to sounds so tiny and dumb to him, like a small, bald man in a suit (his words, not mine!) telling him no. He told me when things get bad at home, like when they have the same argument they've been having for ten years, he wants to go out and blow his shit up. He wants to destroy his whole life.

"What would that feel like," I asked him, "to destroy your whole life?"

"Like freedom," he said.

"From?"

"From everything. From my marriage, obviously. But also from having to pretend like I give a shit about any of it."

*   In 1983, researchers Prochaska, DiClemente, and Norcross developed the transtheoretical model (TTM), which is a biopsychosocial model that identifies specific stages of change when modifying behavior: precontemplation, contemplation, planning, action, and maintenance. While the time inside each stage varies, the tasks required inside the stages do not. James O. Prochaska, John Norcross, and Carlo DiClemente, *Changing for Good* (New York: Harper Collins, 2007).

He didn't mean he didn't care about his life or his marriage. He meant caring about it felt dishonest at times, when what he really wanted to do was submit to the truth, which is life sucks. Being alive sucks. At least it did for him.

I am not unaware of the tremendous suffering in the world, nor am I unaware of my privileged lot in this life. People live in war zones where rape and genocide are weapons. There are hate crimes in our neighborhoods. The ecosystem is falling away species by species, and the people currently running our country don't believe in climate change. Some kids call their friends "gay" to mean weird or stupid. Yet another black kid gets shot dead by a cop while some rich white douche bag gets *nothing* for raping an unconscious woman. I'm a therapist, and I have access to others' struggles, and I absorb them because I love my clients and I'm emotionally invested in their lives.

So you think *fuck it all*. I don't see how anything gets better, do you? At home, you can barely make ends meet financially, and when you feel excited about something, it is soon enough over, or it doesn't work out, at least not in the ways you'd hoped. You think *what else should we do but escape?* Where is the salvation in being here, present, with all the hard things? Where is the salvation in *being*?

One of my main interests as a therapist is how my clients do or don't feel alive, what walls they've built to avoid real, authentic connection. Without human connection, what is life other than a series of tasks we complete to get through each day? Life can be terribly boring. The other day, I went to Trader Joe's for groceries, stopped at another store for toilet paper and trash bags, went home, made some Annie's macaroni and cheese for Griffin, and the whole time, all I could think was *Who cares?* This is so *boring*.

I wanted to help my clients with this feeling. I wanted to help myself.

Eight

I fell into the drums.

MY MARRIAGE WAS A MESS. MY CAREER WAS A MESS. YET when I tried to clean up the messes, I cleaned up the wrong things. I left the messes at home and spent more time out with my friends.

One night, a friend had a birthday party, and I talked Bob into going even though, for the most part, he had learned to stay away from me when I went out and drank. He said he'd go, but only if we left by ten. Eleven, I said. Fine, eleven. Julia, Mitch, Bob, and I drove together so we would have a sober driver. Obviously not me. Obviously not Julia. Probably not Bob.

I drank a lot at that party, not surprisingly. I stood outside with a handful of other people who liked to smoke when they drank, and I went inside only to sing, since my friend whose birthday we were celebrating was manning the karaoke. Where was Bob? I don't know. Probably talking to someone who wasn't drunk. Probably annoyed with me. Probably wanting to go home.

I sang my karaoke favorites: "Edge of Seventeen," "Alone," "Crazy on You." Sometime around eleven o'clock, people began leaving. The first wave of leavers are always the couples without drinking problems. They go home, floss and brush their teeth, and wash their faces, and they get into bed and read. Maybe they make love. When they wake up the next day, maybe they get breakfast together at a reasonable hour, before all the drunks make their way to the brunch spots, eager for some hair of the dog and greasy food. They go hiking. They take walks, holding hands. They work on their gardens. They change their furnace filters. They say things like, *Hey, you want to catch that five o'clock matinee at the film festival?* They are much better at life than I am, and I was certain they are who Bob wanted us to be.

But here I was at midnight, an hour after I'd promised Bob we would leave. Two hours, really, since I'd cleverly negotiated that extra hour. Here I was, singing karaoke to the tune of "If You Leave Me Now" by Chicago but changing the words to "If you make me leave right now, you'll take away my favorite party. Oo-oo-ooh, no, baby, let's not go." I climbed onto Bob's lap with the microphone, entertaining myself and possibly my friends but definitely not Bob. I thought I was hilarious. I mean, I was clearly a witty vixen who Bob didn't deserve.

When Bob finally got me to go, Mitch drove with Bob in the front and Julia and me in the back. They were going to sleep at our house because their place was a solid hour away from the party. She asked, "You're sure it's okay for us to sleep over?"

"Of course!" I said. "We'll have coffee together in the morning."

"What if we hear each other having sex?" she said.

"Well," I said, "don't be surprised if you hear me yelling, 'That's right, bitch! Take it all! You know you like it!'"

Julia and I giggled.

"Bob might be wearing a bunny costume. Don't judge him. It's a lifestyle. His dick wants what it wants!"

We were bent over laughing, practically on the floor of the car. In retrospect, none of this made any sense, but we were drunk and cracking ourselves up. In the front seat, Mitch tried not to laugh, but Bob didn't look so happy.

"Whassamatter, Bob?" I said, snorting. "I'll say anything for a laugh. What's wrong with that? Life is for the living!" Did I say that again? Or did I just think it? Because the only time I felt alive anymore was when I was too drunk to care about anything.

In bed, Bob turned away from me. The next morning, he left early. I texted him around noon: Lunch?

I don't even want to see you right now, he texted back. I'm too mad.

Me: Mad at what? What did I do?

Him: The fact that you don't know makes me even madder.

Me: Is it because I was funny last night? Because I had fun? Do you even like me?

No response from Bob, but I guessed his answers would have been yes, yes, no.

I went to a friend's house to drink and smoke and analyze what happened. I missed the irony, of course, that I was drinking and smoking to deal with my feelings about Bob's issues with my drinking and smoking. So many ironies in addiction. *What a relief*, you think. *I'll stop fighting. I'll just give in.* There's a George Jones song in which he croons, "If drinking don't kill me, her memory will." Isn't it like that? The misery of your life is there whether you drink or not, so you may as well soften the edges.

Bob called to check up on me. "Are you drunk?"

"No," I said.

"I'm not talking to you about this when you're drunk."

"I just said I wasn't."

"Maybe you should stay there tonight."

A sober person might have understood that he wanted me to be safe, to stay where I was because I was drunk. I thought he didn't want to be near me because he didn't love me. I hung up. I stayed the night in my friend's very comfortable bed, thinking I had to end this marriage, because I didn't want to be with someone who couldn't love me.

My life was whittled down to drinking. I was reduced to a person who drank.

I regularly arranged to meet friends at a bar with an outdoor patio so we could drink and smoke long into the

Kerry Cohen

night. I ordered my wine. The bartender asked, "Do you want to keep a tab open?"

My answer: yes. Always, yes.

Then I meandered into the back where the patio was. In the nonsummer months, orange-coiled lights heated the mostly closed-in areas. There were picnic tables. Old ashtrays with black bottoms. I knew some of the regulars and said hello. My friends arrived, first one and then the other, and we drank. Pinot noir was my favorite, because it was thin and crisp. One friend drank gin and tonics, which she'd heard were lower in calories, and the other drank an IPA, which is a kind of beer. Here in Oregon, we have the best microbreweries, or so people told me. I'd never liked the taste of beer, except Corona, which I drank strictly on vacations in Mexico, and even then, only one or two. I kept the idea of my distaste for other alcohol in the back of my mind as a way to limit drinking someday. *Someday.* But not now.

We talked and smoked and ordered more and drank and talked. I liked being buzzed. Just taking that edge off. Just that feeling that I was floating above my list of hard things. But here I was. I went too far, and I was drunk again.

Many women I know have a "thing" they do whenever they're drunk, like a gambler's tell. Julia snuggles up with her female friends and tells them how much she loves them. Emily falls asleep wherever she is (and yes, we've taken pictures, because that *is* funny). Another friend, otherwise hetero, tries to make out with women and likes to lift her skirt and compare cellulite in the bathroom.

When I was drunk, I liked to tell some random guy that if I weren't married, I'd take him home with me. It was terribly pathetic, the middle-aged lady slurring at some hapless twentysomething that she'd take him home if she could. *Oh, yes, please do take me home, crazy drunk lady. I'm so very disappointed you won't.* This was what I did to a guy one night at a favorite bar. He had dark hair and scruff, two features I find lovely on men, and he was holding a pint of beer. He leaned against a beam near our patio table. He smoked. I don't remember how we started talking, but my friends and I introduced ourselves. I didn't catch his name. Soon enough, I said that idiotic thing I say when I'm drunk, and then I went further and told him that he could never have me anyway because I was out of his league. To be fair, I didn't mean his looks. I meant in what I did for a living. And I didn't even mean "out of your league." I meant something more like, "I bet we wouldn't have much in common anyway," but what I said was so awful, so disgusting and cruel, that he turned away, done with us.

"We aren't with her," one of my friends said.

I immediately started backtracking, trying to explain what I really meant. But it was too late. The damage was done. Here's the worst part of what I did: I saw the look on his face when I said it. I don't remember what we were talking about right before that moment, but I remember his expression with great clarity. It said, *she saw me.* I hadn't, really. I was just some drunk, middle-aged woman who spat out some nasty words. But I hurt this man. I must have hit on something painful inside him. Unintentionally, but who cares? Had I not been drunk, I never would have said it.

I saw him later when I went to the bathroom.

"I'm sorry," I said. "I really am. It was a horrible thing to say, and I didn't mean it."

He nodded dismissively. He just wanted me to go away.

We got cut off that night. I had never been cut off at a bar before. But when the waitress came to get our order, she told us no more alcohol. We were done. It was this same bar that cut me off just a few months later when I was gesturing wildly as I spoke to a bunch of strangers whose table I'd joined. I knocked my wineglass to the ground, where it shattered across the concrete. Wine spread across my jeans, making it look like I'd gotten my period hours earlier and didn't care. Just as this happened, the waitress passed.

"Ready for your check then," she said. It wasn't a question.

Another night, I went to see some live music with a small group of friends. When my friends and I got to the club, I went straight to the bar.

"I need a drink," I told the bartender, who smiled. She heard that all night, every night. Everyone needs a drink. I ordered my usual house red. "Cheapest red you have." I grabbed my glass and stood outside because I needed a cigarette too. One glass of wine was usually about two cigarettes' worth. I stubbed out that second cigarette and went back in for another wine. A friend came out to join me for a smoke and then went back inside.

Any bar I went to needed to have an outdoor, heated

patio. If there wasn't one, or if my friends sat inside instead of smoking, I wouldn't see them most of the night, because I'd be outside guzzling drinks and puffing away. I always made friends on those smoking patios. We were like our own tribe. We knew smoking wasn't cool anymore. It was relegated to those who hadn't gotten their lives together. Who had babies but then went right back to sneaking cigarettes on the front porch. Who had divorces and had fallen into midlife crises. Who had isolated themselves again and again. We discussed everything and nothing, mostly making sure none of us were left alone out there. That would feel bad, we understood. That would feel like a problem, and here was one problem we could take care of for each other.

By the time I was on my third glass of wine, my friend came to find me.

"You're missing the whole show!" she said.

"I know." I laughed. "I know that. I'll be in in a second."

The truth was that I hadn't come to watch the music. I had come to drink. But it would be weird if I spent all night out here, and I didn't want to make my friends worry. I sat with them for a while. After my fourth glass of wine, I made my way to the bathroom. The whole bar was soft and fuzzy and just a little off balance. As I passed the band, I knocked into something and lost my footing and fell into the drums. *I fell into the drums.* The band stopped. The drummer helped me up. I could feel that I had bruised my thigh. I didn't dare look back at the room, where everyone was staring at me. Can you imagine? But I pretended everything was just fine. *I meant to do that!* I was desperately trying to make drinking a part of my regular life. This is normal! My bad behavior is normal!

If I got together with a friend, it was to drink. Friends said, "Let's get coffee," and my response was, "Wouldn't you rather get a drink?" About five years into my drinking career, I no longer cared what time of day it was. If it was morning, we could get mimosas. Any time after noon, we could move on to wine.

I sometimes drank in the mornings. "Sometimes" is vague. It might have been often. I mean, relatively often. Compared to most people. I would say I drank too many times in the mornings, because pretty much anytime you're drinking in the morning, it's too many times. I called this breakfast wine. Breakfast wine is found in glasses from the night before. If it's not in your glass from the night before, you might find it in someone else's glass. Very rarely, you will find it in a not-quite-empty bottle. If you're a real alcoholic, you won't find it in your own glass, because alcoholics don't leave alcohol in their glasses. I once heard that a critic condemned the award-winning movie *Ironweed* because in one scene, Meryl Streep leaves alcohol in her glass at the bar, and this, according to the critic, is something no alcoholic would ever do. Incidentally, because I had *plenty of times* left wine in my glass before bed, I hoped this was one more piece of evidence that I wasn't a true-blue alcoholic.

Breakfast wine's primary purpose was to ward off the emotional doldrums that inevitably showed up the day after heavy drinking because, surprise! Alcohol is a depressant. We know this! When you're drinking too much, people often remind you that drinking is likely adding to your depression. It slows your reflexes, slurs your speech, and makes you miserable. Not the night before, of course! Not while you're yelling at the karaoke jockey that you are entitled to one more song before they close because everyone else got to go once more and you didn't. Not while you're singing "Barracuda"—badly— while the DJ, bartender, one server, and your last remaining friend wait so they can just go home and get some sleep. But the next morning, yes. The next morning, you remember how you humiliated yourself and you really need to stop drinking, but first this breakfast wine so you can feel better *right now*. Right now is every addict's favorite time.

I wasn't the only one behaving badly. Plenty of my friends were as eager as I was to drink. My friend Hannah and I came up with Wine Wednesdays. Hannah and I met through a mutual friend, and we quickly and easily grew close. We were both extroverted. We both loved to chat while drinking and smoking. We often invited other women to join us, and they regularly showed up. We met on an outdoor patio at four in the afternoon, because this is Portland, where apparently no one works nine-to-five jobs. Our other friends had one glass and no cigarettes, and they were gone by 5:30. But Hannah and I stayed there through at least two more of both. Usually more. Whenever I'd go to meet friends for "a drink," I said to Bob, "See you in an hour or so."

"Ri-ight," he answered.

When Hannah and I drank, we came up with ideas we

thought were fantastic. One of our first was *Zombie Apocalypse: The Musical.* Another was a female cover band of Tenacious D, called Tenacious V. Our last was a web series about two single, middle-aged women trying to meet men. In it, we would play our worst selves. My character would be a pathetically desperate woman who just wanted someone to love her. Hannah's would be a woman who talked endlessly to men about herself while they tried to get away. We'd pretend to be drunk the whole time, of course.

For our web series, Hannah had this idea that her character would call mine after waking up in the morning. "What are you doing today?" she'd ask my character. "I don't have to work."

"I don't have to work either," I'd say.

There would be a beat.

Then, in unison, "Day drinking?"

We didn't need our characters to play out those scenes. We had *become* our worst selves. Back then, I had counseling clients only on Tuesdays and Thursdays, and on the other days, I should have been writing. Instead, I drank. Fuck it. Nothing ever came to anything anyway. Every free day was an excuse to have fun, and having fun meant drinking. We started at one of the few bars with smoking patios that opened before noon. We knew which ones they were: Beulahland, Lucky House, Bye and Bye, and a bunch of dive bars we loved. Conversation started with laughter, but as the day progressed, creeping toward 3:00 and 4:00 p.m., we'd head into dangerous terrain, which for me was anything to do with Bob. It wasn't just that my friends saw my struggle with him. At least one thought he was self-involved, and he had been outright nasty to a few.

What are you doing with him? they all wanted to know.

I said: *That's what I'm trying to find out. That's why I'm not ready to leave.*

These conversations went nowhere. I'd wind up crying, a sloppy drunk who cried in bars, for God's sake. Like a sorority girl. Like a freshman in college.

Like the drunk I had become.

Nine

I'm killing myself because I can't get my shit together.

ADDICTS USE SUBSTANCES OR BEHAVIORS TO QUIET EMOTIONS, to take the edge off. We engage in most of our addictions to avoid the despair waiting for us when we stay still, when we stop chasing or stop running away. Even before I drank heavily, I spent most of my time concocting plans that involved not standing still, whether I was planning the next vacation or busy with my three jobs. When you stop moving for a moment, the wind dies down, and suddenly it is just you and your existence.

Alcohol was not the first substance I used to take the edge off. Smoking was. That began when I was a child. At twelve, my best friend Liz and I found half-smoked joints in ashtrays around my father's apartment. We thought about trying those but instead harvested the butts of his cigarettes, lit them with matches, and took a few puffs. By the time I was thirteen, I was a full-on smoker. I smoked Marlboro Lights, like my dad, mainly because I couldn't buy them from a store. I took packs from his cartons. I probably smoked about half a pack a day. By the time I was fifteen, I stopped smoking in secret in the stairwell of our building and started smoking openly with my dad. I switched to Benson & Hedges Ultra Lights. I liked how long and skinny they were, which was what I longed to be. Cigarette companies know how to appeal to women. My best friend Amy smoked Benson & Hedges Lights 100s for the same reason.

In the mid-1980s, you could smoke in bars, where they accepted our ridiculous fake IDs. At fourteen, I frequented the West End Bar and the Amsterdam Café, both on the upper west end of Manhattan. There were plenty of fellow prep schoolers from Horace Mann, Chapin, Dwight, you name it. Eventually we moved our evenings to Dorrian's, which was on the Upper East Side. Amy was a year older than I was, and when she turned seventeen, she drove us there in her brand-new Honda Accord. I ordered a sea breeze each night because I could tolerate the range of flavors, and I would sip it throughout the night, the glass sweating in my hand. One drink. No more. But I smoked many cigarettes while we sat there, waiting for boys to find us.

When I left for college, I was still smoking. My best friend there was too, but she felt bad about it. She thought smoking was gross. She didn't like how her clothes always smelled. She was determined to stop, and I secretly hoped she wouldn't. Who would I smoke with if she quit?

Then I met my first long-term boyfriend, Eli. He implored me to quit. Because I was dependent on men's attention, because I would do anything to make myself lovable to him, I did. I was nineteen.

When we broke up, I started again. Then I met Leif and fell in love, and he too begged me to quit, so I did. I didn't start again until we broke up as well. And so continued my cycle with cigarettes. I smoked when single and lonely and trying to find someone to love me, and I quit in order to be loved.

In your forties, when you realize you are not, in fact, immortal, smoking presents a risk more tangible than not being loved. Some nights, I lay in bed, and my heart hurt—literally—and I thought, *Well, here we go. I'm going to die. I'm killing myself because I can't get my shit together.* Balance that against the fear that comes in middle age about losing beauty and sex appeal, and you've got yourself a shitstorm of confusion. When I looked in the mirror, I hardly recognized the woman I saw. I was aging, obviously. Gray hairs had begun to appear, and the wrinkles around my eyes had deepened. I had that crepey, sun-spotted thing going on with my neck and chest. And I was suddenly way too aware of my upper arms.

What I couldn't see and didn't feel was what might be happening inside my body, hidden beneath the surface.

I told this to my therapist, and she explained early versus late stages of alcoholism and how if I kept going, eventually my body would start breaking down. Aging would exacerbate it, and then, the ultimate outcome of alcoholism is death.

"The ultimate outcome of life is death," I told her.

She smirked. I was so hard to work with that way.

Still, her comment spooked me enough that I did a little research. It wasn't pretty. Over time, excessive drinking ravages the pancreas, liver, and central nervous system, including the brain. It leads to malnutrition, cardiovascular disease, and increased risk for a number of cancers. It messes with your neurological health, and it speeds up the aging process. Basically, it has the potential to screw with almost every organ and system in your body, not to mention the accidental deaths associated with drinking.

I went to my doctor and had my blood drawn for a full panel. It all came back just fine. I was an ox! Even my liver was tip-top! But signs of danger had begun, mainly the fact that I often woke in the morning trembling from too much insulin rushing through my body.

Just the other day, my mother, who is in her early seventies, said, "I feel like I was forty yesterday." That shit scared me to death.

The irony, of course, is that both drinking excessively and smoking would end my life sooner. I joked to Bob, "You should see the way women age in my family. They never die. They wind up three feet tall and skeletons with sprouts of hair at 98. We *need* to take years off my life."

But this joke had gotten as old as the others about my drinking and smoking.

Ten

I planned Bob's funeral.

PEOPLE OFTEN CALL MY WRITING BRAVE. READERS SAY, "Thank you for being so fearless." I never know what they mean. Brave? Fearless? My God, what are they talking about? I walk through my life trembling, unable to turn off my vulnerability. And now, the shame about the drinking, about all the people I failed, about how something so damaging got me so deeply in its grasp, it stays buried inside me. I don't want to look at it.

Shame is like hammered metal inside you. It lodges there, sealed forever. Nothing seems to make it budge. Think of a time when you felt truly, deeply ashamed. Do you still cringe a little at that memory? It's awful, I know. I've felt shame often, but my drinking shame had a new flavor. Sour, metallic, sharp.

A friend told me she lied about her drinking when filling out new patient forms at the doctor's office. And also when getting a massage.

"Me too!" I said, relieved I wasn't alone with this embarrassment.

"I mean, why do they have to know how much I drink per week to knead my muscles? Why does it matter?"

"Exactly!"

"Same with sexual partners," she said. "Why do you need to know how many people I've slept with before you give me this facial?"

"What kind of a facial *is* this?" I said.

I was sick of myself, of these tiny embarrassments that snowballed over time. There were little ways I'd begun to take steps toward changing my behavior. The first was an essay I wrote for an online magazine. In it, I examined this notion that I had developed a late-onset drinking problem. I wrote about how I had moved my addiction from love and sex to wine, how they had tangled into an indefinable shape.

Readers' comments came in droves. Half the responses came from people who related and found the writing brave, and half came from people who thought I was an asshole. Maybe both were true. Maybe I was brave *and* an asshole. People are complicated. I kept unabashedly putting my stories out there, not to gaze with love upon myself but to get to a truth that I had hoped would help both me and my readers in some way. Even that sounds arrogant. I don't mean it to. I wrote from a place of self-discovery. I still do.

When I saw those comments people had written, about how I clearly have borderline personality disorder or I'm just a jerk or I'm self-involved, I felt misunderstood.

After the essay came out, friends contacted me, wanting to talk about their own problems with drinking. I felt suddenly exposed. I had put myself out there without thinking it through. I worried clients would see my story. At a literary event a couple of weeks later, an acquaintance said to Bob, "Is Kerry really drinking in public after that essay?"

I could have stopped drinking at events. But I simply went to fewer of them. I didn't need to threaten my writing career any further.

When you're an addict, you lead a kind of double life. One of my clients, who is in AA, told me that she was terribly drawn to the appeal of having a secret life. In a world where everything feels spun out of control, where we all feel so defenseless, a secret gives us power. It's something we can control. My life was so full of vulnerability—as a memoir writer with a book about my sex life, as a mother of an autistic boy—it felt good to have something no one knew the whole truth about, even as it also felt like an ongoing bad idea. But now everyone knew the truth about it because I had bared myself again. What had I done?

One night, not long after the essay had come out, Bob joined me outside. He had been going through a constant back-and-forth with me, trying to find his place. Tonight was one of the nights he tried to meet me where I was rather than be alone. Those were the choices I left him: sit outside with me while I drink and smoke or be alone. He opened a bottle of beer.

"I'm concerned this is the only way we can connect," he said.

"That's ridiculous," I said. "We connect in other ways."

He leaned back in his chair and looked up at the night sky, at the plane flickering across the sky. "How else? Tell me."

"We both like to hike," I said.

"When was the last time we went hiking?"

"We just need to do it more often."

"I feel like you're missing the point," he said.

I could feel the way his body was shutting down to me, slamming internal doors one after another, trying to keep himself safe.

"I do understand," I said.

"Do you?"

"I know what you're trying to tell me."

He sighed, put his head in his hands. "I don't want to live like this anymore."

"I know," I told him. "I know that."

I don't know how long this period of knowing and not knowing has to go on. Elizabeth Wurtzel called it "nondenial denial."* You know you have a problem, a truly bad problem with addiction, but you don't make moves to stop. Or no, that's not true. You do take steps. Small ones. But you don't jump

---

* From her memoir *More, Now, Again* (New York: Simon & Schuster, 2002) about her addiction to Ritalin.

all the way into recovery. I heard Bob that night. I truly did. I knew what was happening even before he told me. I wasn't ready to completely let go of the ways in which my vices kept me safe from my pain. I was choosing my addictions over my marriage, much like what happens in an affair.

"I'm going up to bed," Bob told me that night, and like so many nights before, I let him go alone.

When I binged on TV, I mostly watched shows that made me laugh. Or I watched series that drew me in so deeply, I forgot about what was happening inside our house. Some of those dramas brought up feelings about Bob, feelings about how much I was still in love with him. I wrapped myself inside the idea of him, the fantasy of him, rather than him. It's perverse, really, how we sometimes devote ourselves to the one thing that will get us the opposite of what we want. I always had. During my loose girl years, I claimed to want intimacy but pushed men away with my neediness. Now, I was doing the same thing to Bob with my drinking.

I've always bitten my nails. Bitten them down to ragged nubs, ripped at the skin around the cuticles. I always had stinging hangnails and pain in my fingers, but I couldn't seem to stop. I had acrylic nails put on and redone every couple of weeks, hiding the truth of what was beneath. A polished veneer over a painful mess.

"It's okay," I kept telling Bob about the drinking and smoking. "I'm going to stop."

"When?" he asked. "You keep saying that."

One night, in bed together, we talked for the first time about what I would need to be able to stop. We decided to take a camping trip somewhere beautiful and magical: the Canyonlands in Utah. We wouldn't bring any wine or cigarettes. We'd be so busy during the day with hiking and setting up camp and so taken with the beauty at night, I wouldn't miss them.

We decided we would go for our first anniversary in October. This was in March, which meant I had a full seven months to enjoy myself. Or avoid myself. I also had seven months to try to figure out how I would live without escaping into a bottle.

I told my therapist, Lucy.

"What are you feeling about that?" she asked.

"Honestly," I said, "I think I won't have any problem giving up the wine. I'm *physically* addicted to cigarettes, but I think I'm only *psychologically* addicted to drinking."

Lucy watched me. She was used to my bullshitting by now.

"Well, it might be good to prepare yourself in case both are hard to give up."

"Maybe," I said.

Bob changed his mind and said that October was too far away. He needed me to stop sooner.

"Why?" I asked. "Why do you care so much what I do?"

"What you do affects me. You go off and leave me alone to take care of everything."

"I do not."

Kerry Cohen

Bob threw his hands in the air. "Fine. You don't." And he walked away.

Later that spring, he came outside to find me. He had a beer, and he lit one of his cigarettes.

"I need to talk to you about something," he began.

I poured more wine. Those words rarely led to anything pleasant. I took a breath and nodded for him to continue.

"I have desires for Alex," he said.

Nausea rose in my throat. Alex was one of Bob's closest friends. I swallowed it down with a gulp of wine. I lit a cigarette. I couldn't believe we were still here. Nothing had changed. He still wanted other women. I was still outside with a bottle of wine and a pack of cigarettes, trying to avoid it. Here we were, face to face with our core issues.

"I know," he said, seeing the look on my face. "But I don't want to do what I always do. I don't want to push it down, feel bad, and lie to you. I want us to do it together this time."

"Together?" I asked.

"Yes," he said. "Let's figure this out together."

I wanted that. I wanted us to get somewhere new. It hurt, but I was going to talk to him about this thing that had plagued our relationship from the beginning.

For the next two weeks, we went outside together and had discussions about how to tackle this problem. They were good discussions, about monogamy and open relationships and what we felt we could and couldn't do. I was nowhere near ready to have him be with another woman, but I wanted to get there. I wanted him to have what he needed so our relationship might survive.

"Someday I'm going to regret this," he said. "When you decide *you* want to be with another man."

"I can't imagine that," I said, and I meant it.

At the end of those two weeks, Griffin and I traveled to see my father and his wife, Toni, in New Jersey. When we got to his apartment, I immediately cracked open a bottle of wine and had a cigarette. Traveling was stressful. It was a long trip. Everything was an excuse to drink. My father eyed me warily. I could feel the inclination to hide, to steal away with the bottle and drink it in my room, maybe with the window open so I could smoke, like I used to when I lived there as a teenager. This hiding and guilt are so typical of addicts, pretty glaring symptoms of addiction.

A client of mine, a recovering sex addict, told me a story in which he went to rest in the bedroom and took his phone. He had never acted out with his phone. He used only the computer for excessive pornography watching. But his wife, also recovering from what his addiction had done to their marriage, followed him into the room. He looked up, guilty, ashamed, even though he was doing nothing but checking Facebook.

"Let me see!" she said, her hand out. "Give me your phone!"

He handed it over, and she spent twenty minutes scanning his history but finding nothing. Later, she cried, hating herself for the terrible feeling she fell into when she tried to control what he was doing, her futile attempts to protect herself from more pain.

"Why did you look guilty?" she asked him. "I wouldn't have overreacted if you hadn't looked so guilty."

"I don't know," he said. "I guess because I *am* guilty. I'm a bad person."

I was on my third glass when my father confronted me. "That's Toni's good wine," he said. "She only has two bottles."

"Is there another one I should drink?" I asked.

"Maybe you could simply stop drinking."

This time, I looked him in the eye. I love my father, but sometimes his hypocrisy is too much for me. "Do you want to talk about this, Dad? Because I will. I'll talk about all the things you partook in while I was growing up here with you. I'll talk about who I learned from to become an addict."

He went pale. He half laughed. And he walked away.

That night, I passed his room to go back to the terrace to drink and smoke some more. I smelled weed. The next day, he came home from the Grand Union with five bottles of wine just for me. Not-so-good wine, but good enough to enable me and avoid any more confrontations.

Two days after we arrived, I couldn't reach Bob.

I texted: Are you alive?

Then, two hours later: You're dead.

Three hours later: OMG you're dead.

Five hours: I'm planning your funeral.

I didn't hear from him until two in the morning when I startled awake to the sound of his text: I miss you so much tonight.

Maybe it was because I was half-asleep. Maybe it's

because he'd been unreachable all day. But my hackles went up.

Why tonight? I asked.

He didn't text back.

The next day, we spoke on the phone, and he was strange and distant. I tried to enjoy myself. My father and Toni had taken Griffin to some dinosaur park, something I wasn't interested in doing because it didn't involve sitting on the balcony with a glass of wine in one hand and a cigarette in the other and watching the George Washington Bridge traffic.

When they left, I poured some wine into a to-go cup, stole an oxy from my dad's supply from when he had skin cancer, and went to sun myself by the apartment complex's pool. I brought a book, but I didn't read. I watched a young family visiting grandparents. I listened to their thick Jersey accents as they yelled affectionately at each other. The sounds of my people. I was a Portlander now, through and through, but sometimes I heard that accent or saw a family like this one and considered a different life I might have lived, one where my children would have grown up with those accents, where I might have married a wealthy bond trader and lived in Demarest. I didn't have it in me to be that person, but at times like this, under the hot, polluted sun, I liked to imagine a different life.

I got back to the apartment before my family did, so I stepped outside for one more smoke. I had been out there so much on this trip, I had come to know the flight patterns of planes, which seemed to come just about every five seconds from various parts of the sky. When my family arrived home,

I was on the couch, reading my book. I had just come in from outside, but I looked up, smiling, like, *Oh, well, look at me doing what I always do, which is something responsible I should be doing and not drinking and smoking on the balcony like the lush we all know I truly am.*

That evening, Michael's sister and her daughter came to see us. I sat with my sister-in-law (I would never call her my ex-sister-in-law; I love her too much) on the balcony with the lit-up bridge and cityscape as our view. I always delighted in having someone who liked to drink and smoke, even if her drinking and smoking were much more moderate than mine. Griffin and my niece played a board game inside. I didn't hear from Bob all night. The next morning, ten eastern time, seven back in Portland, he texted me: I'm sorry I've been horrible to you. Do you have a minute to talk? I had barely written back that I did before the phone rang.

"Listen," he said. "Something happened."

I knew immediately. I realized I'd known all along. I hung up, unable to handle it.

I love you I love you I love you, he texted. Please don't go away.

For the rest of the day, I wanted information. No talk about how it affected me yet. No endless apologies. I wanted to know what exactly he and Alex did, for how long, where. They didn't even kiss, he promised me. There was no inter-course. He gave her a neck massage while she drove, and that somehow led to them getting each other off while in a moving car. They were both regretful, remorseful.

All I could do was picture it, the two of them, eyes forward, their hands down each other's pants.

I drank, and I cried. All that day, I drank and cried.

How had I gotten here? Crying in New Jersey, Bob apologizing about an indiscretion in Portland, this damn wineglass always in my hand. I was sick. I was literally and undeniably sick. Something was horribly wrong, and I wasn't sure how to change it.

Between drinks, I walked through a haze, trying to take care of my son as best I could. Mainly, I focused on getting through moments, one and then the next.

When we got off the plane in Portland, Bob drove Griffin to his dad's, and then we went back home. We sat in the backyard and drank and smoked and tried to figure out what the hell was wrong with us, and how, if at all, we would be able to heal.

Bob and I went to couples counseling. The therapist's office was a large room, big enough for a couch and easy chairs *and* a desk and bookshelves, I noticed enviously, on the top floor of an old building in downtown Portland. Our therapist was a gentle, compassionate man who had a first name for a last name. I told the story of what Bob had done. *What Bob had done.* That's how I spoke about it. Bob stayed quiet, letting me talk, but I could see the muscle in his jaw jumping.

"What about you, Bob?" the therapist asked. "What's happening for you right now?"

"That's her experience of how things went," he said.

"Really?" I said, furious. "You have a different way

to talk about how you did this horrible thing to ruin our marriage?"

He looked at me evenly. "There is more than one way to ruin a marriage."

My mouth twitched. He meant my drinking of course. The night I returned from New Jersey, he asked me what I needed to overcome his cheating. He'd do anything, he said. I told him I needed them to not talk for a while, not forever, not even for a long time. Just two weeks. I needed two weeks during which I wouldn't wonder if every text that came in was from her, when I wouldn't wonder if every time he wasn't with me, he was with her.

Two days later, on our way to a friend's house with the kids, he sulked in the passenger seat. His energy was a wet blanket in the car. "What?" I asked.

"I miss my best friend."

The following night, he asked me to go for a drink to talk. We sat outside, but the sky was overcast, and I could feel the start of a drizzle. I lit up a cigarette, trying to prepare for what was coming.

"I can't do it," he told me.

I blew smoke out in a thin stream. "Do what?" I asked. "Which thing can't you do?"

"I need to be able to talk to her. You have your friends to talk to right now, to tell them everything you think I did to you. I don't. She's my best friend, Kerry. And I don't see why she should suffer."

In just days, that anger had come back. His voice carried

with it that same resentment it usually had. Little digs about things he was pissed about. His anger that I talked to my friends about the ways in which I felt he hurt me. He believed I turned people against him.

"I don't know what you want me to say," I told him. I was so sick of crying, so exhausted by this same conversation, by his desire for other women, by his putting other women's feelings before mine. I didn't want to have to fight to be loved, to be chosen above the others. If I didn't have most of my glass of wine left, I would have stood up and left him there. But I did, and I needed that fucking wine right now.

I went to Julia's place the next Saturday. During the weeks Bob and I had all four kids, it was something I could do with them that was inexpensive and allowed me to drink and smoke all day with my friends. Bob didn't like it, but his kids had lots of fun there, and if Griffin was going somewhere, they often wanted to tag along. Bob grudgingly agreed to let them come. He stayed home, as usual, and I left Ezra there, since he preferred to be in his own house. I once asked Ezra, long ago, if he ever wanted to travel, and he said, "I want to stay in Portland, my country." That's how small he preferred to keep his world.

We drove the twenty-five minutes to her place, and the kids ran in. It was like a second home for them. Julia's house was one of those places where children were welcome and happy. She always had lots of kid-friendly food and beverages—hot dogs and pizzas, juice boxes and Popsicles. The playroom had all the toys any child could want, and games for the Wii and

Xbox. The television had all the kids' movies cued up, anything they might want to watch.

I joined the adults in the backyard under the gazebo and began drinking.

I was there maybe an hour when Bob texted: Alex wants to come over to help me with the yard, and since she wants to work on it, and you obviously don't, it would be great if you can be ok with that.

I took a big breath and let it out slowly. The yard was on his long list of things I didn't do enough of or didn't do the way he wanted. And Alex, his Achilles pussy, wanted to help! I was exhausted by the hurt, and the slight buzz I was working on didn't help much.

I wrote back: Do whatever you want.

Him: ok, thanks.

Me: Just make sure she's gone by 4:00. I don't want to have to see her.

Him: I will.

Me: You're an asshole, you know.

No response.

I poured more wine in my glass, tried to focus on my friends. I tried hard not to imagine what might be happening at home. Tried not to rant on and on about him to my friends. I was struck with the realization that this relationship really had ground me down to my worst self.

When I pulled up to our house, it was 8:00, and yet there was Alex's car. People don't often think of trauma as something that occurs outside of war or rape. But our brains experience even the smallest things as trauma. A parent yelling too often at her child, or getting bitten by a dog, or your partner engaging in infidelity—all these teach your brain that, when faced with something associated with that thing that happened that felt so awful, you will move into fight, flight, or freeze mode. This is what happened to me when I saw her car. It felt like a punch to the stomach. I had to remind myself to breathe. And I had to get the children safely inside the house before I lost my mind, which was what it felt like was about to happen.

Inside, the house was dark. I checked on Ezra, who was playing games in his room, and then I walked slowly upstairs to the master bedroom, my throat constricted, my breath not right, afraid I would find them there, in Bob's and my bed. But they were not there. Where were they? In another room? Were they here at all?

I texted: You left Ezra here alone while you left with your affair?

I heard nothing for fifteen minutes.

Then: We're here. Out back.

Out back? *Out back?*

I realized I was hyperventilating. Then I started crying.

I poured wine, got my cigarettes, and took them onto the front porch. I was panicking. I was decidedly not okay. I needed help. I called Hannah, who said she would be at my house in ten minutes.

Later, she told me she called Julia and Naomi to ask their advice about whether she should do this. She knew Bob didn't like her. She was one of my many friends who he felt had an obnoxious personality. And she knew if she came to help me, with the plan being she would go to the backyard and simply ask Alex to leave, Bob would dislike her even more. She might wind up banned from the house, as some of my friends already were, according to his rules.

Hannah arrived. She hugged me. She told me later she could see how dire this was, that I was shaking, and my face was streaked with tears. She knew there were children in the house who weren't being attended to. She knew I wasn't functioning and that she'd made the right decision to come.

"I'll be right back," she said, and she went through the house to the backyard.

What happened next comes to me only through the people who were back there, and they all told very different stories.

Here's the thing: some stories will save you, and some will release you, and others will lead you to believe what you most need to believe. I will never know what truly happened, but I was also desperately tired of beating on the chest of a relationship that simply would not live.

Hannah found Bob and Alex. Bob was drunk. Empty beer bottles crowded the table. Bob's daughter was draped across the two of them, sitting on Alex's lap with her feet on her father's legs. Later, Hannah said she saw what she knew I would have seen: a family with Bob that didn't include me, as though he were grooming Alex to be the new stepmother.

Hannah told his daughter to go inside because she needed to speak with the adults. Once she was gone, Hannah told Alex she needed to leave. She told her I was inside, feeling unable to go into my own backyard because she was there, that I was hurting because of what she and Bob had done while I was in New Jersey.

Later, I would learn from Alex she had no idea I had been struggling so much with Bob's infidelity. Bob had told her I was fine with it all. I still don't know what is true, and I never will.

Alex said she would leave, and as she gathered her things to leave, Bob told Hannah she had no right to tell his friend what she needed to do, that this was his house, and that *she* was the one who needed to leave.

Hannah said, "Your wife is in there hurting, and I'm the only one who seems to care!"

What happened next is debatable. It's debatable because Hannah told me one thing, and Bob told me another, and in the end, I had to make my own determination about what was right. Because it wasn't just the details of this evening that mattered; it was the aftermath. The ripple effect from this night probably affected Bob's and my relationship more than the actual events.

I heard Bob yelling. That I know. Soon after, Hannah came back to the front patio. She was breathing heavily, clearly shaken. She told me Bob had stood up and gotten in her face. She was scared, and reacting from childhood trauma that included a rage-filled father, she pushed Bob back into his chair. He stood up violently enough to knock over the chair. Then—and this is the thing he most vehemently denied—he poked Hannah in the chest.

I saw the red spot on her chest. That's something else I know. Alex later said she didn't see what happened because she was busy righting Bob's overturned chair.

Alex left, and Bob went inside. Hannah and I heard him tell his daughter I was jealous of Alex. It was dawning on me, a slow spread, that everything was horrible, that things between Bob and me were irreparable, and this scene between him, Hannah, and Alex was over-the-top crazy.

When Bob and I finally talked about it, he said about Hannah, "Who does that?"

I said, "I'm sorry, who does *what* exactly?"

Bob said he didn't want Hannah coming to the house when he was there, which is exactly what she had feared.

I was tired of hurting, of losing people I loved, of feeling like there was something wrong with me.

I still didn't see the connection to drinking.

Eleven

I quit drinking for a week.

NOT TOO LONG AFTER BOB AND ALEX HAD THEIR DALLIANCE
in the car, I left for ten days to teach at the low-residency MFA
program where I was faculty. Low-residency means that the
faculty and students meet for ten days, twice a year, to teach
and learn from workshops and plan for the coming semester.
One of my colleagues and I shared a house, a beautiful short-
term rental that was owned by an artist couple. The house was
all blacks and pretty greens and ceramics. The backyard had a
pond with adorable koi that came rushing to the edge when
people came by, hoping for food. I wanted to appreciate it. I
intended to. But by the third day, we had completely trashed
the place with empty wine bottles and beer cans and coffee
cups overflowing with ashes and cigarette butts.

I kept thinking *someone doing better than me deserves to be staying here*, because I was not doing okay at all. I woke every day around eleven or noon. I made coffee. Sometimes I showered. I thought often of exercising. That would be good! I didn't eat. Around one in the afternoon, I started drinking and smoking. I avoided texting Bob who, when I did text, answered with one or two words. Very rarely did he contact me first. He was angry with me because by his own choice, to appease me, he had asked Alex not to join him on a camping trip while I was away. I felt like I was being punished, but for what, I didn't understand. Wasn't he the one who had cheated on me? So what if I drank too much! Couldn't he have some compassion that I was doing my best? The pain between us was still so raw. The awareness of that was like a clammy film on my skin. I buried my days at the residency in wine and cigarettes.

One night at a bar, I stepped outside to smoke, and a fed up twentysomething bouncer followed me and grabbed the wine out of my hand.

"Hey, fuck you!" I yelled. Then, to my friends, "Fuck this place."

We moved on to the next place, but when one o'clock in the morning hit, a couple of servers told us we all had to get out.

"I can't finish my wine?"

"Not unless you want to get arrested."

"What is wrong with this town?" I yelled. I slammed down my drink and stomped from the bar.

Another night, we gathered in the backyard of the rental house, and I stood up, pointed my finger at one of our students, and verbally destroyed him for suggesting gay men were female inside.

I was losing it, one drunken day at a time. Not quite what the AA people had in mind for that maxim.

By the fifth day, I woke in my room, shaking and weak. Briefly, I worried I had become a late-stage alcoholic overnight, but in reality, I was eating next to nothing and drinking so much sugary wine that my insulin was on overdrive. My housemate tried to feed me an egg, but it was undercooked, so I threw it out. I lit up a cigarette instead.

Usually at these residencies, I'm engaged and social. But this time, I holed up in that house. I made people come to me. My workshops were lacking, nowhere near what my students deserved. A student complained to the director that she thought I was drunk during one of my seminars. (I was not! I was hungover! That's completely different!) I loved this job, and if my fellow faculty and director weren't good friends who were actively worried about me, I easily could have been putting my job at risk. Something had to give, so I researched some options.

If I went to rehab, I could leave everything at home. I could sleep a lot and sit in support groups with other women and complain about my problems. The women would nod their heads, so understanding. We would go on walks, and I'd probably lose some weight. But I couldn't leave Michael with the kids that long. I crossed off that idea. Besides, it's one thing to live like that for a month. You still have to come home to whatever you live with daily.

I am stubborn. I don't like it when people tell me to do things like everyone else does. When Michael and I first understood Ezra was autistic, I hated the pressures put on our family, on me especially as his mother, to do certain things. He's autistic? Oh, well, I hope he's in occupational therapy. He's autistic? Oh, well, I'm assuming you've given him dolphin therapy. I assume you tried glutamine and omega-3s. I spent the first five years of Ezra's life holding my arms out, elbows locked. Back off! I wanted the whole world to back the fuck off while *I* figured out who my son was. Not the doctors. Not the speech therapists. Not his teachers. Not some concerned stranger in the grocery store. He was my son, and I wasn't a complete idiot. And even if I were, I still had a right to my own process of discovery as a mother. It was still my life and my son's life, and it was no one else's business what I did or didn't do for my son.

This is how I felt about my drinking. I didn't know yet if I was an alcoholic or a problem drinker. I didn't know yet if I had to go to AA or if I could do something else. I didn't know yet, and I wanted to find out on my own terms. People don't talk about that very much, but recovery, however you define it, is personal. It's private too. How I went about helping myself—and how much I stumbled along the way—was my own business.

If there was a time when I had absolutely no relationship to alcohol, then why shouldn't I be able to go back to that? Lucy said no. Alcoholism is a progressive disease, she argued, and denial is the disease of alcoholism. But she assumed I was an alcoholic, and I thought I wasn't. Almost everyone I spent time with was also overusing alcohol, my friends in particular. They had never been heavy drinkers before either. If I was an alcoholic suddenly, then we were all alcoholics, and that seemed unlikely. I thought it was more likely that we had all come to places in our lives that we didn't know how to handle. We had been worn down by life's discomforts, small and not-so-small.

I began to research harm reduction, also called moderation. The moderation movement offered a plan: give up drinking for one month. Reintroduce alcohol, just one or two drinks, only a couple of days a week.

A few of my clients were secretly trying to figure out whether they could moderate after having been in AA. Secretly, because the pressure in AA to (a) never doubt the program, (b) never leave the program, and (c) never, *ever* think you have control over your addiction makes it scary to speak aloud.

One of these clients was young, only twenty-four. She had gone to AA because her mother gave her an ultimatum—either she went to rehab or her mother wouldn't support her financially. She went. But now, about five years later, she didn't think she had a problem anymore. Her drinking and drug abuse had been situational, developing only after having been date-raped. She drank half a glass of wine one night. She did the same a couple of weeks later. When I asked her how she thought it was going, she said, "You know what? I don't think I even like it anymore."

Another client had gone to AA in her early thirties after too much drinking, too much drugging, too much sexing, too much of everything. Now, fifteen years later, she was furtively drinking wine again and smoking cigarettes. She admitted that she'd been using them both too often lately. Members of her family were sick, and she'd been traveling about six hours almost every weekend to help care for them. A few months later, her family stabilized, and she stopped drinking so much. She decided to quit smoking, and she did that too.

There were people, however, who did not have success stories. They drank again and learned quickly that they couldn't do so with any control. I knew plenty of people who had stopped drinking but smoked loads of weed. Others took pills. And some who avoided substances altogether ended up struggling with their love and sex addictions or eating disorders. Focusing on the *thing* instead of the emptiness is a waste of time, but it's easy to make that mistake if we assume that addiction is simply a disease of the brain.

If you look for it, research is abundant. Most heavy drinkers are *not* alcoholics, meaning they can change their behaviors with alcohol if they choose to. I'm not making this up! The National Survey on Drug Use and Health of 138,100 adults showed that nine out of ten people who drink too much are not actually dependent on alcohol.* Physical dependence is present when neurons adapt to repeated exposure to

* Tara Parker-Pope, "Most Heavy Drinkers Are Not Alcoholics," *New York Times*, November 20, 2014, https://well.blogs.nytimes.com/2014/11/20/most-heavy-drinkers-are-not-alcoholics-study-finds/?mcubz=3.

a substance and can only function normally when the substance is present. When the substance is withdrawn, the user experiences several physiological reactions. This is withdrawal syndrome. In the case of alcohol, withdrawal syndrome can be fatal, so true alcoholism is not something to mess around with.

In addition, according to newer research, alcoholism is not necessarily a progressive disease. The National Epidemiologic Survey on Alcohol and Related Conditions found that about twenty percent of alcoholics wound up being able to moderate over time.[†] And alcoholism is not an either/or prospect; it's a continuum, with most people on the mild or moderate end. People who drink heavily don't necessarily need to become sober, and—I hope you're sitting down—they don't need AA.

I would do it. One month. I could do one month! I knew, at the very least, I needed to try.

When I arrived back in Portland, I told Bob my plan. He was thrilled, and he offered to do whatever it would take to support me. I told lots of people. I figured the more people I told, the better. Most of my friends congratulated me. We had been talking about this for so long.

The night before I started, I drank a bottle of wine. This was nothing new. I had been polishing off a bottle a night for a while now. I sat outside, watching *Parks and Recreation* on

---

[†]   Gabrielle Glaser, "The False Gospel of Alcoholics Anonymous," in *The Best American Science and Nature Writing 2016*, ed. Amy Stewart and Tim Folger (New York: Houghton Mifflin Harcourt Publishing Company, 2016), 84.

my computer, and smoked half a pack of American Spirits. I allowed myself this last bit of depravity. I didn't want to think much about what was to come.

That first morning of sobriety, I woke with a slight hangover, which was not the best way to start. With a hangover, my body wanted to drink again. I wasn't going to give myself the option this time. I stuffed down the thought, took the kids to school, did some work on my computer, went to a coffee shop, did some more work there, picked up the kids. It was around four o'clock when I started to think about wine. It wasn't time to make dinner yet, so I went upstairs and tried to read. Nothing kept my attention. At five, I made dinner. At six, I started to think about whether I really needed to do this sobriety thing. One month? Was I crazy? Who cared if I drank a little bit! Lots of people have a couple of glasses with dinner, a few cigarettes after. I counted in my head the people I knew who did that: one of my sisters-in-law, two of my friends, a celebrity I'd read about. Didn't George Burns live until he was one hundred drinking scotch and smoking cigars every day of his life?

I got my kids to bed, got my own self to bed. I lay there, tossing and turning. Maybe I could sneak one, I thought. I could get up and be like, *Oh, just checking to make sure all the lights are off.* But if I was the one trying not to drink and smoke, exactly how was I going to hide this from *myself*?

The next day was the same. And the next. Every day that week from four until nine, my brain played out a discussion about whether I could have just one drink, just one smoke. What was the big deal? As though having that brain discussion didn't signal a problem. I mean, were people who didn't have a drinking problem arguing with themselves every night about whether they could have a drink?

Without the filter of alcohol, everything took on a new level of irritation. Bob and the kids spilled crumbs everywhere. Four children in the house couldn't stop moving their bodies. Everything anyone said made me want to peel the skin off my face. Bob still took three showers every night, still used every towel, including the hand towel, because all the other towels were still hanging over the bed. His toilet habits rose to a new level of disgusting. Everyone chewed so loudly, I was sure the next-door neighbors could hear it. Griffin complained about anything and everything, and Ezra banged out rhythms on the wall that reverberated throughout the house.

None of this is terrible or unique, but all my willpower was being used to avoid drinking and smoking, and I had little left to handle these minor nuisances in my life. Had I not been drinking so much, so regularly, for so long, I might have handled these annoyances with finesse. I might have rolled my eyes and hunkered down and done the things most grown-ups have to do. I can blame my inability to handle anything on the shitshow that was our relationship, on this dysfunctional blended family. I can blame it on some tendency I have toward addiction or on some weakness in me. Whatever the reason, my life had become intolerable without it. A drink, I thought. One fucking drink could make this okay.

But I stuck with it…all the way to Friday when Bob and I handed off the children to their other parents.

"It's our free Friday," he said, referring to what we called these two best Fridays of every month.

I love my children. I always missed them. But that first Friday night was pure bliss. It was, hands down, the best thing about being divorced.

"We can have just a couple," I said tentatively. "We deserve it!"

"What's wrong with having a couple of beers?"

"Or a couple of glasses of wine?"

"We'll go home at nine," he said.

I didn't say anything about the fact that I was supposed to be abstaining or that he had been so thrilled that I was. Maybe, as much as he had thought he wanted the change, he found out he didn't want to have to change with me.

We drove to Mississippi Street, the anticipation fluttering in my throat. In the summer, Mississippi is Portland idealized. Young hipster couples with their children in graphic tees and cute dresses walk hand in hand. Salt & Straw serves artisan ice cream. Twentysomethings and fortysomethings comb through vinyl in record stores to play on their vintage LP players. As we walked to a bar, one that had a patio of course, I thought of who I used to be, a young mother, never thinking even once about a drink. A younger single person, still solid in my belief that I would wind up happy, in love, with a successful career as a writer.

We ordered a cheese plate and a beer and a wine. I didn't think about the idea that I had been planning to change all this, that I had been teetering on the edge of a new direction. I didn't think—or I didn't want to think—about what it meant that I was drinking now. Because it meant that nothing would change. Bob and I would keep walking down this path of destruction. We would not manage to fix our shitty relationship or our unworkable family. I focused on the relief of this old habit between us, which was to submerge all our problems in alcohol, to soften and mute them until they were faded enough to ignore.

A couple of men sitting behind us had American Spirit cigarettes, and they made me tell them a joke when I asked if I could bum a smoke.

Why did the mushroom go to the party?

Because he was a fungi.

Why did the fungi leave the party?

Because there wasn't mushroom.

They weren't that impressed, but I got my cigarette.

Soon, though, I walked to a nearby market to get my own. I threw a cigarette down on their table and smoked eight from my pack. Drank four glasses of house red. Made Bob talk to me again about the night he betrayed me with Alex so I could feel the pain and fury, so I could play out our old drama, feel it fresh and real, so I could feel alive inside it. This was a constant push-pull. I didn't want to feel the painful feelings, but I also didn't want to feel dull and numb. Bob tried to change the subject. He didn't want to go to painful feelings at all.

The next morning, I woke up and puked. My headache was like a jackhammer in my skull. I drank again for hair of the dog. And then again. And just like that, I was back on track with my drinking.

Twelve

I didn't have to go that far.

IN THE FINAL YEAR OF BOB'S AND MY MARRIAGE, MICHAEL and I went to a beach house with our children. He was supposed to go with his girlfriend, but they had broken up. Breakups can feel devastating, unrelenting, and without reprieve. He didn't want to go alone, and I didn't want him to be alone either. I knew we'd be drinking while we were there. He was in pain, which at this point in my life, maybe his too, called for the need to numb and escape. How do well-adjusted people grieve a relationship? Michael liked beer and white wine. I liked my red wine, and he brought a box to thank me for coming with him.

Bob came along because he didn't want me to be alone either—with Michael. He didn't trust me with him. Maybe it seemed dangerous to him? I don't know why. Michael and I were solidly "just friends" and had been for years by then, but Bob didn't trust me with much at this point. I had never given him a reason not to trust me around other men. I was in love with him, and he was the only one I wanted. I assume his mistrust had more to do with my drinking than anything.

Bob had gotten pneumonia recently and had stopped drinking and smoking for a little while. It turns out illness can be a great tool for changing habits. He had a beer here and there, but now it wasn't a regular nightly activity for him. He would drink too much again eventually. He would smoke again too. But for that month, he slowed down, and he was in a nice, smug place to let me know how much he still resented *my* drinking and smoking.

On the drive out, Bob and I argued about the things we always argued about now: my drinking and smoking and what Hannah had done the night Alex was at our house and I was freaking out. We were so predictable at this point, and we were both exhausted.

At the beach house, Michael and I drank and smoked and talked about his breakup. He believed that at his age, no one would want him. Michael is, for lack of a better word, a catch. He's kind, smart, and hilarious, and he has two wonderful children about whom I might be biased. He had no reason to believe that no one would want him again, but this is what we do. We tell ourselves our stories, and we cling to them like gospel, and then everything seems to be evidence in service of our narrative—like me with my consolation prize story. I tried to talk to him, to remind him of his value, but sometimes it seems impossible to hear anything other than what you believe in the moment, and this was one of those times for him.

Michael and I knew each other better than anyone else. We had gotten married at twenty-nine. I had believed with my whole heart that this would be it. I would finally be happy. I wasn't completely foolish. I knew that life still brought hardships, but I believed that having a partner I loved would make everything easier. We bought a house. I planned our wedding. I worked out daily and lay in the sun, browning my skin so I'd look fantastic for the wedding. I had a job running a writers' center. I lounged in my backyard with a faint self-satisfaction about how my life was moving along exactly as I'd planned.

Michael was completing graduate studies and working a full-time job. He was anxious about his life, and he struggled to stay positive. Back then, we had few real worries. We had parties in our backyard. We laughed a lot. We talked about our future. He knew I wanted to have a baby right away, and though he didn't really want the same thing, not yet, he nodded along. A friend of mine used to tell me I was like a dog with a bone when it came to things I wanted. Michael didn't even try to talk me out of it. Sure enough, soon after the wedding, I got pregnant. I threw myself into the pregnancy, just like I had the wedding. I bought books. I joined message boards. I diligently swallowed prenatal vitamins. At ten weeks, Michael and I met at my gynecologist's office to see the heartbeat. On the screen, there was no movement, no beating at all. There was only a tiny seed, measuring six weeks from when it had died. I had to pee, and the cruelty of that need felt unbearable. If I peed, that would mean I moved, and if I moved, then life would really be happening. I couldn't stand the thought of it, of sitting on a toilet, of the crude humanness of peeing.

For the next few months, I walked through my life as though I were a ghost. Everything brought me grief—the cashier from whom I'd bought the prenatal vitamins, babies, pregnant women, car seats. Miscarriages are like breakups. The loss is reflected everywhere. When I spoke to a friend about how badly I seemed to be taking it, she told me it was because I'd always been charmed. Everything always seemed to go my way. Maybe she was right, but it was more than bad luck. Since my mother left when I was twelve, this was the first time I had experienced such a loss.

I have always hated that feeling of being out of control, of not being able to get what I set out to get. When I was in my twenties, I wanted to be a witch so I could control things. I bought books and herbs and tinctures, and I tried focusing my mind to make things happen. I was never a fan of trying to stay still while the world swirled around me, hurting me as often as it did. As a child, I built superstitions. If I get up the stairs in under ten seconds, nothing bad will happen. If there is no car coming down the street right now, I will get my wish. For a while, I really did believe. I tried to be intentional in my desires. I tried to create my own reality. I did love spells on men and money spells, always ending them with the phrase "No harm be done" so nobody would die. In the end, I controlled very little, because the truth is we can't control much.

I did get pregnant a few months later with Ezra, but something had shifted. I no longer felt sure everything would work out. For the first time, I realized that life would unfurl however it would. This was the beginning of life chipping away at how I'd thought it would go, the beginning of its gradual erosion. And so it was that Ezra wound up on the autism spectrum, and then Michael wound up depressed and withdrawn, and then nothing made sense anymore at all. I didn't drink back then. Instead, I had that emotional affair. Depression, affairs, drinking—they're all just ways of not being present.

Sitting and talking to Michael on the beach, I saw how we'd faced real challenges in our marriage and yet here we were, at the coast together, still part of each other's support systems. I wondered how Bob's and my marriage would withstand any real obstacles, problems we hadn't brought on ourselves.

Bob was asleep by the time I got into bed. We had been in this constant loop where he woke up at six or seven and started writing. I woke up around ten. He was asleep by ten in the evening, while I sat outside with my wine and cigarettes. By the time I got into bed, he was always asleep. We hadn't been having much sex. We'd barely had physical contact. I might put my arm around him, press my cheek against his neck. He'd shift a bit, sometimes take my hand, but eventually, he'd roll away.

In the morning after breakfast, I went to the beach with Michael and the boys. Before we left, I poured some wine into a coffee cup. In the kitchen, I turned around, surprised to see the boys had followed me. I saw the confusion on Griffin's little face.

"Just getting some wine," I said, smiling. "We're on vacation!"

He smiled back, his face calm and trusting again. Sometimes, the key to not hurting someone with your addiction is to not hide it. The saying goes that alcohol is like a truth serum, but the opposite was true for me. For the past year, I'd found progressively sneakier ways to hide my alcohol and tobacco use from Bob. I said I was going to the store to pick up milk or dinner. I snuck out other times to buy wine, hoping he wouldn't notice I was gone. I lied about how much I drank, and I lied about how early I started and whether I was drunk, especially if I had been driving. I knew all this. I knew that I was lying and hiding and telling half-truths, something I hadn't done since I was a teenager trying not to get caught doing stupid shit. I hated dishonesty. I had spent most of my life trying to get as honest as possible with myself about my relationship to men, and now here I was again, practicing deceit.

As much as I hated myself for lying, I did it because I felt guilty and ashamed. On some level, I believed Bob when he said there was something wrong with me—with my drinking, with my parenting, with my behavior at parties or around friends. We'd both been hiding things from each other, though neither of us was very good at it. The fact that he even confessed to cheating with Alex when I was in New Jersey didn't mean he was being completely honest. There was more to this story that would unfold, and one night, I got a sneak preview that made me rethink so much of the dysfunction in our relationship.

A mutual friend was having a book-release party, and Bob was in the bathroom, messing with his hair. I could feel some strange energy coming from him. Was he nervous? Tired? Angry with me again?

"What's the matter?" I asked.

He shook his head.

"What?" I said. "Tell me."

"She's having the after-party at Cassidy's."

I didn't understand. "And?"

"She's having it there to make a point," he said. "Because I got so drunk there at my fortieth birthday party."

I'd heard stories about that party. He had gotten well and truly drunk and, in his words, had made an ass of himself, and he had obviously been carrying around that embarrassment for years.

If a cartoon lightbulb with a terrified face could have appeared over my head in that moment, it would have. There had been many times Bob told me how people were plotting against him. Local writers were interfering with his writing career and his ability to get published. A handful of people were trying to get him fired from a job. Someone hacked his email account, which he knew because messages were disappearing.

He had been so convincing about these scenarios, I had not understood they were part of a much larger pattern. If he was so wrong about the book-release party, about the author's motives, what else had he been wrong about that I had believed? For the first time, I understood I couldn't trust him as much as I had, and perhaps it was time to start trusting my own gut.

Later that fall, as promised, Bob planned the Canyonlands trip. He thrived on that sort of thing—planning trips. I think many people do. Vacation planning is all about the fantasy of what will happen, that you'll be relieved from daily life and its stressors, and you'll find some new balance while gone.

We flew into Salt Lake City, rented a car, and got on our way. We discussed the billboards that aimed to call people to Mormonism, so alien to our own beliefs and lifestyles. We admired the beauty of the southeastern Utah landscape. These were ways we could still connect, and they mattered a great deal to me, maybe even gave me hope.

At the trailhead, we put on our packs and headed out. We had a seven-mile hike to get to our campsite. The terrain was desert that had been carved long ago by the Colorado River. It was magical, full of natural, surprising, sculptural structures. We climbed out of canyons and back down. Scrambled up rock faces, following cairns to stay on the trail. Sometimes we talked, discussing our writing or our life dreams. Other times we stayed silent, taking in the beauty around us. We had not been like this—peaceful and connected—in ages, and I appreciated every moment. After many hours, we found our campsite. Bob was an experienced camper, much more so than I was, and he was happy to take the lead in setting up our tent and making food. He was effectual at this, which was different from all the ways I felt that he flailed at home, unable to focus on anything, unable to follow through, and therefore so often frustrated with himself, with his life, with the ways I wasn't helping. Perhaps that's because camping was really about survival, getting from point A to point B. We need *this* for shelter, and now we need *this* to eat.

As the sun set, he reached into his pack.

"I brought a surprise," he said, and he produced a flask full of rum.

I didn't like rum, so I didn't partake, but Bob took a few shots, and soon we made our way into the warmth of our tent, where we made love, something we hadn't done in a long time.

"I've missed you," I whispered before we fell asleep.

The next day was the same. We hiked to see some of the famous structures in the park, and we gasped at the splendor, shaped by nature's hand, before calling it a day.

"I'm impressed with you!" Bob told me. "You aren't complaining about the hiking." He meant the steep inclines and deep drops. There were times we had to sit on our butts and shimmy our way down the rock face.

"Why would I complain? I love this!"

We read books we brought, lying side by side in silence. At night, we watched the moon come out, and then the stars, like lights turned on. I didn't have any desire to drink and only slightly craved a cigarette.

On the final day, we hiked seven miles back to the car. It was a relief to get there, but I couldn't help but feel a little blue. Our time in the Canyonlands had been so good, so different from our day-to-day lives. For those few days, I felt connected to him again, and it brought into relief how much that was no longer the case for us. I knew it was unlikely we'd maintain this intimacy, as much as I hoped we would.

Indeed, gradually, imperceptibly, our relationship fell back into its natural place—he would want other women, and I would drink too much, and we would never again recover the magic we absorbed from that enchanting national park.

If I had to pinpoint the end of Bob's and my relationship, it would be during this time. He was done with my drinking. I was done with his desires for other women. It's easy to point fingers. *I started drinking because you wanted other women! I was miserable with you because of your drinking!* How many more times would I do this punting of blame with a man?

Sometimes the solution is to get out of each other's way so you can finally acknowledge your own lifetime's cache of carefully curated unhappiness. I have a theory about relationships: we are attracted to specific people because those are the people who will hand us the best opportunities to love ourselves better. Those people will unwittingly know the best way to poke at whatever triggers we have, not to hurt us but to offer the chance to take care of ourselves better than we have before. In this way, all relationships, no matter their pain, are gifts. The gifts might feel like burning shit in a bag, but they're still opportunities for growth. Fucking growth. Enough already with growth! It never ends, and it can never be easy. But if we must assign some sort of meaning to life, I think this might be it.

In bed one night, I opened my laptop and looked up

rehabs. Maybe I could find an intensive two-week program somewhere so I wouldn't have to leave my kids for too long. Bob leaned over to see what I was doing.

"Rehabs?" he asked.

I glanced at him. "Isn't that what you want?"

"Well, no," he said. "I don't think you have to go *that* far."

So that was a relief. I didn't have to go that far.

Thirteen

I met someone.

Midspring, I met someone. If you didn't think I was an asshole before, here's your chance to rethink that. When Bob eventually found out, he certainly thought I was an asshole. But Bob and I were so far gone. By then, we had hurt each other so many times in so many ways. We have both admitted that no one had ever hurt us worse than we hurt each other. We were involved in this terribly addictive relationship, one where he wouldn't choose me, and then he did, and then he wouldn't again. And I stayed and stayed for more. To this day, Bob would insist that I stopped trying because I met this other guy, but I was just *ready* to stop trying. I was looking for a reason to stop trying. And that's the painful reality.

I was still drinking too much, and people who drink too

much don't tend toward responsible decisions. If I could go back now to this time, I would have ended things right then with Bob. I would have asked for a divorce that very day. I would have told him I'd met someone else and wanted to move on. But I can't go back, so here's the ugly truth about what happened.

The same weekend I met this man, Bob told me he didn't know if he loved me anymore. I cried, but I was ready to be done, and he gave me one more excuse to be done for good. Soon after, I told Bob I wanted to separate, although it would still be some time before we both committed to the end.

This new guy. Let's call him Kyle. Let's call him Kyle, because that's what he said I should call him. Kyle said I should describe him as a tall, black man with a big dick. He wasn't black, but he wasn't exactly white. And he had a big dick. I'll leave it at that. I'm going to keep him anonymous, not just because one generally does in memoir, but because—and here's where you're going to really hate me—he was married. We were both married when we met. And, oh my God, it gets so much worse, but please stay with me.

We met through a friend, and one night, we were at the same bar. We ordered drink after drink, and I told him how unhappy I was in my marriage. Isn't that original? He, however, told me very little about his wife. At one point, she called, and he left the table to take the call. By then, we had already established that we were interested in a possible sexual relationship. I drank pints of cider, and by my fourth pint, I asked him the size of his dick, and on his third pint, he told me. We made plans to email each other about getting naked together.

After that night, we spoke solely through secret emails. At first, I told him, "I can't do this. I can't have a secret email. That's disgusting. Only horrible people do that!" Two days later, I was checking those secret emails regularly, writing nasty, sexy words back to Kyle, who was writing nasty, sexy things to me. I was completely comfortable with my new secret life. That's how quickly we can head down that road. Or that's how quickly I did.

Despite all the ways I'd been hurt by Bob's desire for other women, his choosing their feelings over mine, and his furtive behavior, I had entered the same world. I was sure I was done with Bob. It was just a matter of time for him to find his new place and get out.

Meanwhile, I drank every night. Every single night, I sat in my backyard with my computer and my wine and smokes, and I communicated with my new secret lover, and I waited until Bob was asleep so I could sneak unnoticed into our bed.

Every other day or so, Kyle and I met up. We fucked in a church parking lot against a tree. We fucked on a blanket in the park. We made out on the nude beach and then fucked in his and his wife's bed, still gritty with sand. He looked into my eyes during sex and said, "Tell me you love me," and even though I didn't yet, I said it. "I love you too," he replied. Later, he explained this was dirty talk for middle-aged people, and that's when I knew Kyle was a fucking genius.

We went away together for overnights, soaked in hot tubs, fucked again and again, and slowly—no, rather quickly, actually—we started falling in love. Kyle treated me in ways

I'd never been treated before. Here I was at forty-four, two marriages in, many lovers behind me, and no man had ever told me things like "every last thing about you is lovable," "if you were just a brain in a jar, I'd still want to spend all my time with you," and "I'd follow you into battle for your cheekbones alone." I mean, men had said things approaching this here and there, but it felt like Kyle worshipped me. All. Day. Long. After six years with a man who had literally written a pros and cons list about me to decide whether he should stay with me, this was pretty fucking nice. He didn't judge me for my drinking or for anything else, really, and that was pretty nice too.

At home, nothing improved. In fact, now that I had something to compare it to, I grew even more impatient about moving along the separation. Also, something was shifting. I don't know if it was the therapy with Lucy. I don't know if it was having a man treat me the way Kyle did. I don't know if I was simply exhausted by my own doubts. Maybe a relationship that made me feel worse than I ever had before, like the one I had been living with Bob, was exactly what I needed to finally come out of this. Maybe this was Bob's gift.

Through it all, I drank. Mostly, I drank with Kyle, and other times, I drank alone, and every once in a while, Bob came outside to drink with me, and he said, "I fear this is the only way we know how to communicate anymore," which was likely true. I didn't dare talk to him anymore about my drinking. By now, he hated me for it. He wouldn't touch me, because he was so disgusted. Even a year later, still arguing about what each of us had done to harm the other, he said,

"You have no idea what it was like living with an alcoholic who wouldn't budge about her drinking." Whether I was an alcoholic or not isn't the issue. He was right that I wouldn't budge. I wouldn't budge, because his need for me to change my ways was exactly the kind of thing that was keeping me from changing my ways. I don't mean that I was reacting to him like a stubborn adolescent. Rather, his unhappiness with me, his utter inability to be supportive of me or to have any compassion, left me feeling just as lonely as he was, and this is *the thing* that keeps the addictive drive in overdrive.

According to Gabor Maté, MD, in his book *In the Realm of Hungry Ghosts*, which I'd come across in my ongoing research on drinking, people need three things for addiction to occur: "a susceptible organism, a drug with addictive potential, and stress."* *Stress.* That word should have been in neon. Stress is a main factor in addiction.

There are countless stressors in life, and we can't avoid them all. But psychologist Bruce Alexander has found evidence that the most common stressor that causes addiction is the basic desire for connection, something many of us seem to be missing.[†] If you do even the most cursory research on addiction, you will come across Alexander's Rat Park

---

*   Gabor Maté, *In the Realm of Hungry Ghosts: Close Encounters with Addiction* (Berkeley, CA: North Atlantic Books, 2010), 139.

†   B. K. Alexander, B. L. Beyerstein, P. F. Hadaway, and R. B. Coambs, "Effects of early and later colony housing on oral ingestion of morphine in rats," *Psychopharmacology Biochemistry and Behavior* 58 (1981): 175–179.

study. Alexander and his colleagues built an inviting, natural environment for rats in their laboratory. It was about two hundred times the square footage of a standard lab cage, airy, comfortable, and sociable. They created a tunnel that accommodated one rat at a time, leading to two dispensers. One contained morphine and the other an inert substance, both dissolved in a sweet liquid. The animals in Rat Park had little interest in the morphine solution. Even if they were forced to take the morphine for weeks and then made to experience terrible withdrawals without it, they opted not to use it. The caged rats, however, were twenty times more likely to consume morphine and develop addictions to it.[*]

What's astonishing about the Rat Park study is that its findings were published in 1981, when there was already evidence in circulation that social isolation increased addictive behavior in animals. Since then, there have been numerous studies suggesting again and again that some environments are likely to lead to addiction in animals, but that given different conditions, these same animals will not only resist addictive substances, but they will also stop using substances they had previously seemed to be addicted to.[†]

Yet look at how we deal with addiction in our culture. We

Kerry Cohen

---

[*]   Bruce Alexander, "The Myth of Drug-Induced Addiction," testimony given to the Senate of Canada Special Committee on Illegal Drugs, https://sencanada.ca/content/sen/committee/371/ille/presentation/alexender-e.htm#TOP.

[†]   Read more details in Maté's book, *In the Realm of Hungry Ghosts*, especially in chapter 12.

treat addicts as if they're bad people. We punish them. We put them in jail! If we can learn just one thing from Alexander's study, it's that addicts need compassion, not incarceration. They need kindness. A sense of community. When a person abuses a substance or activity, something is wrong in their life, but *the person* isn't wrong.

We assume that addiction is solely a brain thing. It's true that all addictive behaviors act on our dopamine, which is the "feel good" neurochemical in our brains. Some drugs or activities inhibit reuptake, and some increase dopamine.[‡] If addiction were a result of brain activity alone, however, it would follow that any addict would not be able to stop if she started using, and the addiction would only get worse. According to these studies, *that's not always true.* Likely, that's not even mostly true! This blew my mind. Almost everyone around me referred to my drinking as a problem, something I needed to quit. Some of my friends had begun to pursue sobriety on their own. One began an intensive outpatient program. Another went to AA meetings. They had become sober, and they assumed, as it seemed everyone else did, that this was the only way they would be able to be okay.

Many years ago, a good friend of mine got sober in rehab. Before that, when she was still drinking heavily, she was staying with her mother in New York. Her marriage was falling apart. She was having an affair with a man who was

---

[‡] You can find out more about how addictive behaviors work in various places in the brain. Chapter 13 in Maté's book focuses on it.

also married. (Hey, we're a dime a dozen!) Her mother said to her, "I don't know if you're drinking because you're depressed or if you're depressed because you're drinking."

One morning, my friend woke up and left her mother's apartment and went straight to a bar. She ordered a vodka tonic with a twist of lime. (My friend was a classy lady. She still is.) She was texting with her lover, who said, "What are you doing right now?" She said, "Looking for answers at the bottom of a glass of vodka." Something like that. She probably said it in a much more dramatic way. Drinking has a way of doing that, of making you feel as if you're on the stage of a powerful, maudlin play, and everything is dreadful.

My friend went to rehab and quit drinking, and she goes to AA meetings often, and her life still sucks. I can't tell you how many times we've sat together, her with water or coffee and me with wine (I was not being an unsupportive friend; she promised me she didn't care), while she cried about what was happening in her life. She often looked at my glass and said, "I would kill for one of those right now." But she has stuck to her sobriety because she knows that, while it would give her a bit of respite, it wouldn't change anything long term. In fact, it would make things worse. Alcohol is her drug of choice. It is her core addiction, so it is the thing she wants most and the thing that will most surely destroy her life. Addiction is the cruelest conundrum. It is proof there is no God. What kind of a God would make so many of us desire most the thing that will finish us quickest?

I have the same problem with men. When everything

is shitty, I crave the intoxication of a man desiring me. I have to keep myself from texting a certain someone who is bad for me, or I have to force myself to stay put in my house with my children instead of heading out to a bar to find men I might seduce. I force myself to sit with the bad feelings.

Our culture embraces a lie about addiction: when you stop engaging with your addiction, your life gets better. Says who? According to whose life experiences? I wish it were true, but it's so patronizing and unhelpful. What if you stopped drinking, and now you spend so much time exercising and obsessing over your body, you won't have sex with your husband? What if you stopped smoking pot, and now you work until eight every night and you can't remember the last time you had a real conversation with your teenaged children? You don't become better than someone else or a better version of yourself simply because you quit doing something that was harming your life and now you just do it another way.

I'm not suggesting that people who have gotten sober should have taken any other route. Probably they did need to quit drinking for good. Maybe they had had a long history with alcohol that went back to adolescence. Maybe they made terrible choices while drunk, blacked out, or put themselves in harm's way. Maybe they slept with friends' husbands or woke up not knowing where they were or how they got there. Maybe they simply knew alcohol was keeping them from engaging with life the way they wanted to. If their choice was to become sober, nobody should be questioning that.

What I am saying is that sobriety wasn't the only answer

for me. I hadn't had any prior relationship to drinking. I had never had any truly addictive relationship to substances at all. I had a reasonable shot at an alternative, especially if I changed my environment to one that made me happier.

It seemed to me that what we know about addiction is much less than what we don't yet understand. I had known for more than a decade that my core issue wasn't substances. Before I understood that my boy craziness had turned into a sort of love and sex addiction, I thought I didn't have an addict's brain. I had dabbled with so many drugs, including alcohol, and nothing but cigarettes had stuck. Even with cigarettes, I could, for many years, quit and come back to them and smoke only a few occasionally. My core problem was always about love and sex, and substances had served as symptoms of this larger issue. I was certain that if I could get to a new place in my recovery with love and sex addiction, I could change the role drinking was playing in my life.

Meanwhile, Kyle and I stopped at Trader Joe's and 7-Eleven to load up on booze on our way to the beach. We drove along the same forested highway I'd driven when I'd gone to visit Bob and found those condoms. We entwined our fingers, drew circles on each other's knees. In the tiny coastal town, we waited in a mom-and-pop lunch place for service for too long, until we decided life was too short for waiting. We grabbed a blanket and the box of wine we'd bought, and we made our way down to the sunny beach. One can't always lie on the beach in the sun in Oregon. Often, it's too cold or windy or rainy. But we had lucked into a perfect day.

We lay next to each other, sipped syrah, and talked like we had since day one, like there would never be enough time to say everything, like we had been born for this moment, for the ways in which our conversations flowed with ease and meaning. If anything was going to make me happier, I couldn't imagine it. In later months, my body would literally miss his body, the contours of us together, his scent, even his breath. I had spent my life addicted to the expectation of being loved, to the possibility of finally being grounded by a man's desire for me. This was something else, something pure of need or desperation. It was a love I'd never felt before. Later, he told me that it was then, sitting on the beach together, the sun hitting my hair, my eyes lit with desire, and the way our words wrapped around one another's, that he knew he was in love. During sex that night, he said, "Say, 'I'm yours.'"

"I'm yours," I said.

"Say you are all mine."

"I am," I said. "I'm all yours."

God help us.

Here's some advice: don't do what I did. Don't start fucking a married dude before you are out of your own marriage. Don't spend lots of time with the married dude. Don't exchange hilarious and intellectual and sexy secret emails. And for fuck's sake, whatever you do, don't fall in love with a married dude. It was too late for me, though. I was a goner. The sex and love chemicals in my head—all dopamine and oxytocin—had completely taken over any reasonable behavior. When Bob eventually learned about it, as people always do, he said, "How could you do that?" My only answer: How could I not?

Bob was to move out September 1. He was not keen on this turn of events, but it was too late for me. Having been given this new experience with Kyle, a fog had cleared, and a light had been shone on just how miserable I'd been. I didn't know if I could make it until September. That's how clear I was. I considered taking my boys and renting a beach house until then, just so I didn't have to live with him anymore. I know how awful this sounds. Let's just accept together, dear reader, that this is one of the chapters in which I am undeniably a jerk. I don't know how to explain my sense of doneness any better than I know how to explain why I stayed as long as I did. But when I was done, I was *done*. And this was that time.

Bob, feeling me go away, tried a few more times to get me to reconsider. But I wouldn't. I couldn't. The day he moved out, I felt relief. It would be a long time before I felt anything other than pure relief. I could finally be myself without the constant awareness of his determinations about who I was, who I needed to be. I'm willing to consider this was projection to some extent, but by that time, we were so entrenched in our ugliness that I couldn't see that.

The worst part of this timing was that Bob's mother had been ill, and during all this chaos and loss and confusion, she died. The evening he got the news, I'd been planning to leave the house to go to a bar. I had been desperate to get away from the house, from him and his judgment, from the kids, from my life. I was about ten minutes from leaving when his father called with the news.

"Please don't leave," he said. "I need you."

But I did.

I went to a local bar by myself. I made new friends. I laughed and drank and smoked and got drunk, and I will always regret that I did. To this day, I try to understand what happened that night, how I could lose my humanity. I don't want to blame it on the drinking, because that would be too easy. I could blame my behavior on cravings, but I refuse to do so. This is how much I hated myself. This is how much I hated my life. This is how addicted I truly was, not just to wine, not just to Kyle, but to ugliness. If a relationship is supposed to make you a better person, this relationship with Bob had utterly failed.

The day after Bob moved out, Kyle left his wife. I brought him back to my place, and we spent days together, just the two of us and my kids. He began the process of deciding what to do next. I have a photo of Kyle propped up on pillows in my bed, a glass of red wine in his hand. It's hard for me to even look at this photo now. I had so much hope for myself inside those days. For the first time, when he left my presence, I knew he was coming back. He was all mine.

Oh, and we drank! We drank in bars. We drank in my backyard. We drank in my bed. I opened my bedroom window and smoked out my window so we could stay naked and wrapped around one another in my bed.

One afternoon, I went to the store, and when I came home I found him sitting at the edge my bed.

"What's the matter?" I asked. "Why do you look like that?"

He looked sadly at me. His wife was pregnant.

Fourteen

I wished I had a different story.

To change our habits, we have to get sick of ourselves. We have to get so tired, so bored of the same shit over and over again that the only option is to take a different path. I wish I had gotten there sooner. I wish that on the night Kyle's wife told him she was pregnant that I had found the strength to step away from Kyle even though I was in love with him. I wish I had stopped drinking, stopped smoking, and started focusing on all the things in my life that I had neglected—my health, my work, my kids. There were so many things I was sick of. I was sick of having to think about which store I should not go to for another bottle because I had just bought a bottle from them yesterday. Because God forbid the nineteen-year-old cashier think I had a drinking problem. I was sick of making up lies to said nineteen-year-old about how the box was for a party and not for me to enjoy by myself over the next three to four days. I was sick of worrying every time I saw a police car that I'd get pulled over with a glass or two of wine in my system. I was sick of worrying about running into clients at bars. I was sick to death of all of it. We all need to get sick of ourselves, and then we have to go another year or so of being that sick of ourselves, and then we have to get even sicker, until finally, something clicks.

I was also sick of loving men who chose other women's needs over mine, sick of repeating this pattern again and again. I mean, a married man. Really, Kerry? How old did I have to get before I finally figured this one out? It was one thing to be a hot mess in your twenties. But I was in my forties now. I was getting wrinkles and gray hair. I wasn't as pretty, and being wild wasn't nearly as charming as it used to be. I joked often that I was going to wind up alone at a bar in my fifties with a middle-aged hairdo and mom jeans, trying to flirt with younger men. The more likely this got, the less funny the joke became.

I suppose it would be appropriate if things between Kyle and me got worse, but they only got better. We came to like each other somehow even more, to want each other even more, and to have even more fun together.

I was still drinking every day, usually starting around four or five. Wine o'clock. Of course I was drinking every day! I could finally do it without Bob judging me. I could finally live my life without worrying what Bob thought about anything. I figured I'd slow down soon enough, but for now, I was like a freshman in college finally released from my parents' rules.

But home? Home was like the devastation after a hurricane. Ezra was fine. He was relieved to have the chaos of all those extra people out of the house. But Griffin was not doing well. Sometime in the spring, while I was cavorting with Kyle and Bob and I were disintegrating, Griffin started showing symptoms of anxiety. He had always had some social anxiety, but once the summer began, his stomach hurt so much, just at the thought of being around other people, that he had stopped leaving the house. He lay on the couch in the den, television on, holding his belly.

I found him a therapist, and once a week, we drove twenty minutes to Lake Oswego to see a young, good-looking man who talked to Griffin about his fear. The therapist taught him coping skills, while Griffin nodded along, always a good patient. Afterward, we got pizza at a restaurant around the corner, and we drove through traffic to get home. He went back to holding his stomach on the couch. We tried herbal remedies. We tried discussing his life. We tried taking him to the park, visiting friends. Nothing worked. Finally, near the end of the summer, after much consideration, we put him on a low dose of medication, and he got better.

I don't know for sure the severe spike in his anxiety was due to what had happened at home. I can't help but assume, though, that my bad behavior caused it. My son suffered from the ways in which I couldn't remove myself from that terribly addictive, harmful relationship. My son suffered from the subsequent excessive drinking and smoking and general avoidance of life. He did. And that awareness was like an anvil to the stomach. That guilt and horror with myself was some of the worst I'd ever felt as a parent. And that pain, as wrong and ironic as it is, was part of what kept me drinking. I wasn't ready to look this truth in its ugly face.

One night, I met Bob at a bar. He had been drinking for a little while. He asked me if I'd had sex with someone else, and I told him for the first time that I had. I didn't tell him I was in love. Not yet. But over time, drinking together, I told Bob more and more. Through a mutual friend, he figured out who it was, and then he found out about the pregnant wife, and this is when he started sending me texts and emails that were so mean, I eventually had to block his ability to contact me. He called me a sociopath and a narcissist, and he insulted my children for how they looked. I know every relationship has two people. Every argument has two sides. But I had never in my life had anyone talk to me the way this man whom I'd once loved did. He said I was a horrible, evil person, that I deserved to suffer more than I had. Everything was a chance for him to rail at me. When I asked him to return my family's Christmas ornaments he took from the house. When I asked him if he wanted to pick up something I'd found that seemed like a sentimental object. He turned every exchange into a reason to remind me what a piece of shit he thought I was. I wrote terrible, hateful things back to him. We were poison together.

In an attempt at closure, we had a drink after filing for our divorce. Not fifteen minutes passed before he called me a sociopath, stomped off, and left me to pay for his beer.

I cried, and I drank, and I vented to my friends who wanted to help me but were so tired of hearing the ways Bob had hurt me.

"Don't talk to him anymore!" they all said. "You got rid of him! Stop letting him do this to you!" They were upset by his hypocrisy and cruelty, but they were even more upset by my inability to fully let go. God, isn't everything like this? You struggle and get stuck, and you let go, and then you cling some more so you can struggle some more. Changing behavior is like getting rid of packing peanuts. You try to get them into a Hefty bag, and half of them cling to the box or the floor or your clothes. And then you still find three more in the house a week later.

I wished I had a different story. I looked back on those six years with Bob, and I wished I'd never met him. I felt like I'd lost years to my goddamn addiction to men. Years? My whole goddamn life. I was disgusted about it, and I was disgusted with myself. Bob had an entirely different story about our time together. Of course he did. All we have are our stories, the sense we make of our lives. Lidia Yuknavitch, one of my favorite writers, says, "I'm not the story you made of me." She means that we get to claim who we are, and we don't need to be defined by what other people think we are. I tell my clients that they get to change their stories if they want, and this always surprises them.

"How do you do that?" one asked.

"By looking more closely at *your* experience. By not letting anything outside you define you," I said confidently, as though I'd successfully done that in my life. But I *was* determined to. I was.

One of my clients was a porn addict. He used porn to avoid his life, and more importantly, he used it to try to convince himself that he wasn't really a weak guy who wanted to submit to others. He was a mechanic, a big guy with muscles. His friends, he told me, expected him to be strong and manly, and his whole life, he'd been haunted by the fact that he knew he was weak. When I pushed further for him to define his sense of being weak, he clarified that he felt there were entire parts of him that weren't all that masculine, that were soft and sad and wanted to be cared for. This feeling plagued him. He was who he was, but he believed he had to be someone else, so the porn became both a way to avoid the constant, painful conflict he walked around his life with and a way to live out his submissive side, getting turned on by "sissy porn," where men submit to other men sexually. He was trapped by his story, one where he had to be something he wasn't, and that story had led him to addiction.

Change your story.

There's the story you're handed, and then there's you.

This is where I began to change my story.

Well, not quite yet. First I had to obsess about Kyle and his wife and their impending baby. Then I had to lose him because of that, cry deep, gut-wrenching sobs for months until I was hoarse. I had to look at how my story with Kyle was yet another addictive relationship, one where I wouldn't ever get my needs met. *Then*, though. Then I began to change my story.

Fifteen

I refused to stop believing love was magic.

THE LAST TIME I'D BEEN TRULY SINGLE WAS WHEN MICHAEL
and I had separated. At that time, I went through a string of
men—seventeen, remember?—with the plan to let myself
do whatever I wanted with whomever I wanted, no strings
attached. I had sex with a married man, got peed on by a
twenty-five-year-old soldier on leave from Iraq, got it on
with the guy doing construction next door, and sent personal
porn to another military guy in Iraq. I learned a ton about
myself in the process, but when I asked one of my editors
what she thought of another memoir about my sex life post
Loose Girl, she said, "No one is interested in grown women's
sex lives."

Here I was again, single and with a new slew of experiences

no one wanted to hear. Listen, ladies of the eighties. I'm going to lay down some hard truths. When you get to middle age and wind up single, you must consider lowering your expectations. For one, every age-appropriate man is either married or in the middle of a separation, and if you don't jump on it *fast* when he's separating, he will be gone into another relationship. Men do not do well alone, as much as they do a great job of trying to convince us that they really need their freedom, babe. They don't want to get tied down, because there may be a supermodel out there who wants to get with all this. As much as they believe these things, the second they are single, they freak out and need to find a woman so they don't feel sad and unimportant. That way too they can keep believing that if they were only single, they would be doing all those things you keep them from doing. (Hahaha, come on, men! I'm kidding! *You're very special.*)

You can also dabble in the age inappropriate. Post Kyle, I did a few times, all in my desperate efforts to get over him. Here's some more dating advice: *nothing* will go well when this is the impetus behind the dating. One of the guys I met would text every few nights at two in the morning: Ugh. Just that: *Ugh*. This was a sign! He was telling me exactly what was true about what would unfold between us, but I wasn't listening. At some point, I asked him to get together just for sex. No dinner, no date. He clearly wasn't much of a conversationalist, he was hot, and I had no reason not to. He said, "I feel like I need to stop this. I'm not being respectful to you. That's not who I am." Stop *what*? Writing "ugh" at two a.m.? What was it going to take for a girl to get laid in this town?

The next guy was happy to sext constantly for three days. On the third night, he invited me over. For sex. I brought a bottle of wine, but we didn't even get it open before the groping started. It was going great until he started talking, which was almost immediately. I don't mind dirty talk, not in the least. But this was something very different. He referred again and again to my womb, how he wanted to put babies in there. How someone else had beat him to it, but now it was his turn. He called me "mama," and then "mama bear," and in the final throes "yeah, yeah, mama bear."

Then there was the man who wanted me to dominate him. That is so completely not my thing, but after a few text exchanges about it, I thought maybe I should try it. I was, after all, a therapist who specialized in sex. We communicated through texts and phone calls. He called me mistress, and he liked to do things "for me" to himself. I tried it. I really did. But over time, all I got were endless dick pics and photos of his asshole. If he had wanted just once to come over and clean my kitchen floor while I called him a slutty whore, I might have given it more time.

Another time, I had great sex with a guy, and afterward, he couldn't stop smiling.

"What?" I asked coyly.

"I totally made you squirt," he said.

I didn't have the heart to tell him that I'd just peed a little.

For a while, I dated a fortysomething guy who stayed

most nights at my house because he did not, technically, have anywhere else to sleep. He was a sweet guy, but we had so little in common, there was no relationship in our future.

I continued to drink. A lot.

I did my best to focus on my life. Everything was in disarray. My work—my three jobs!—badly needed my attention. My finances were a mess. I hired a cheap personal assistant to help me amass more clients and promote my books. I started drinking tea instead of coffee. In therapy sessions with clients, I thought that tea bag tag hanging over the side of my coffee cup made me look healthy, like, *oh, look at me drinking* tea. *I'm so not someone who makes bad choices.* When Griffin's friends came over after school, I tried to stay inside and clean rather than sit outside drinking and smoking like I usually did. I got a little rush when I heard one of his friends climbing the stairs from the basement playroom, like they would see me washing dishes and think, *Gee, Griffin, your mom sure is responsible.*

During months that followed the loss of Kyle, I learned more about my problems with love addiction than I ever had before. There were deep layers to my addiction. I had been sure that I had conquered the addiction before I'd married Michael, when I thought I'd finally stopped believing a man's love would save me and make me worthwhile. But this was just the tippy top of what I was gradually coming to understand was going to be a lifetime challenge. Addiction is not just one thing. It is not just the thing you ingest or engage in behaviorally, and then you stop, and you're all better. It is not just the triggers and outcomes and relapse and investigation of the childhood that got you there. It is not the drink, the needle, the sweet relief. It is a deeply layered spiritual problem. It is a human problem. It is the fact that we live in a world where no matter how much we love ourselves, no matter how much we go to meetings or do yoga or fast or get acupuncture, these things will not make us meaningful. Quite the opposite. We live in a place where we are always aware that we are not enough. The new car, the new face cream, the perfect pair of shoes—these things are always flashing themselves at us saying, *See? You need this to be worthwhile. See? You still aren't good enough.* I dropped through that first layer of my addiction, and after Bob, I dropped through into finally believing myself lovable, and then I had another layer, which was my longing for Kyle, one person who hadn't chosen me.

When Bob was gone, the universe gave me Kyle as a way to challenge my beliefs in my lovability. Lucy calls this the universe's central casting. Sometimes I think the universe must be a mean girl. You know the type—those girls from high school with the beautiful hair and the cruel smiles and the laughter that cuts like a razor blade. Bob said once in one of his many nasty emails after we split that he hoped someday I would suffer. Someday! As though our entire relationship hadn't been my suffering! As though my whole life hadn't been built upon the suffering of my childhood, of my parents' suffering, of all the human suffering! He got his wish, because nothing cut deeper than losing Kyle.

Listen, I'm not an idiot. It's not like the signs weren't all there, the signs screaming COMPLETELY AND

UTTERLY UNAVAILABLE, that delicious sign that draws in love addicts like hungry infants. He was *married*. He was having a baby with his wife. Any fool could have seen I was bound to lose. But sometimes things happen that feel more important than rationality. One of the definitions of a love addict is that one has "immature" beliefs about love. This includes the belief that love is more than just an economical arrangement. It is more than just negotiating who takes out the recycling and whether you match well due to algorithms on dating sites. Immature love, according to the literature on love addiction, includes believing love is magic. Only people who gave up on the awe and mystery of life would write such a thing! I mean, love *is* magic, isn't it? Aren't we entitled to magic? Still? Even as middle-aged women, even after two divorces and children and failing careers and wrinkles and sagging everything, isn't this what love is *for*? Must we give up everything to be "mature"?

After Kyle was gone, I was a ghost. I tried dating. I tried sex. I tried to burn him out of me with sex and wine and fun. Every last one of those experiences felt like sandpaper. Nothing could replace what I'd had with Kyle. In the past, I could get another dick on the fire and bury my grief in that. This time, being with other men felt worse than being alone, because each of them only dug at the ways in which they weren't him. For the first time in my life, when a man I'd had a good time with wanted to see me again, I didn't want to. Being with anyone other than Kyle hurt too badly. I had to be alone.

This was Kyle's gift. Early on in Kyle's and my

relationship, we tried sex magic. Don't laugh. I know it sounds crazy. Our sex was already magic. Everything between us already felt like magic. But one night, we went into a closed-for-the-night park with candles and a red scarf and images of our chosen deities in our minds. Kyle decided what we'd manifest: new story. New stories. Boy, did we both receive exactly that. Everything inside me railed against my new story. Everything in me wanted my old one back. But I set myself on a course, and there was no turning back. Be careful what you wish for, that mean girl says. I wished to be whole. I wished to be loved. I wished to love wholly. All of these things were coming straight for me, if I could only accept the form in which they came.

This is how you quit love addiction. You decide you want to get better, you wish to get better, and then everything you could possibly need to get better comes for you, whether you like it or not. Counseling helps. Workbooks can be useful. But all you really need to do is pay attention. The world gives you every opportunity to look at yourself, to question yourself, to consider your choices. I refused to stop believing love was magic, because life was so obviously magic too.

Sixteen

I went to an ashram.

THE NIGHT OF THE 2016 ELECTION, I WORKED UNTIL SEVEN.
My last client was a young woman struggling with a family
legacy of suicide. We said goodbye, certain of how the evening
would end. I had invited a bunch of friends to my house with
the idea that we would watch the results, gathered together
around the television. The children would learn about the
electoral college and the importance of swing states. And of
course, we would happily drink wine and sneak outside for
cigarettes. In the end, we would laugh and hug and celebrate
our first female president.

That night sure as hell didn't turn out as I expected! I
never made it into my house after I pulled into the driveway
and got out of my car. Outside my back door was a pathway

littered with wet leaves, and I stood there while people came in and out. I didn't talk to friends who didn't smoke, unless they came out to announce depressing updates.

Later, I went into the garage, now dubbed "Adult Bar" by my friend Amelia, aptly named because it was such a caricature of adult behavior gone wrong. There were at least five empty wine bottles, four empty boxes with the bags inside pulled out like an animal's bladder ripped from its body. These were squeezed dry except for the few drips of red still there. The ashtray, a tiny ceramic bowl Ezra made when he was six, was predictably overflowing, ashes all around it. I lit the garage with a broken lamp, salvaged from the many items stored there. I used old dining room chairs for seating.

By the time Hillary made her concession speech, I was a bottle and a half in and nowhere near ready to call it a night. If I did, I'd have to wake up the next day, and there would be the granddaddy of all hangovers. Most of my friends had left, but I didn't care. If the world was officially ending, I was going down with it. The last two election nights had been so exhilarating: our first black president, and then his reelection. It was impossible to understand how we had been there and now were *here*, how so many people could be this hateful or, at the very least, ignorant. We were sick. Our whole country was diseased, and it was impossible to not feel the weight of that disease. It was impossible not to feel like one sick cell inside myriad sicknesses.

I didn't see Griffin until the next day. I don't know when he went to bed or if he brushed his teeth. I came downstairs in sweatpants and socks, hair frizzy, black mascara smudged under my eyes. I had woken that morning as I figure many people had: with a start, and then that slow, nauseating realization about what had happened the night before. Griffin was at his computer, playing a video game. He turned when he heard me.

"How are you, Mommy?" My sweet, grown-up ten-year-old. He knew what the election meant. He knew about misogyny and racism and all the ugliness the election results represented. He also knew I hadn't been doing well. He knew I drank too much. He knew I was still grieving Kyle's loss. He had been there these past few years, just being a kid, while I had grieved a second marriage, wept into pillows, escaped outside each night to drink myself out of it all.

"I'm not great," I told him.

He nodded. "I know."

I said, "I know you know."

Perhaps what felt like the beginning of a geopolitical apocalypse to a liberal like me wasn't the best time to plan for self-improvement, but it was time. I had no choice.

I had been thinking for a little while I could go somewhere that was not officially a rehab. Based on what I knew about AA, that didn't seem the right path for me. I wasn't a joiner, and I still wasn't sure what I wanted to happen long term regarding my drinking. Even though my first attempt at moderation had failed, I had a feeling it was because I wasn't really invested. This time, I wanted to do it for *me*. Not Bob. Not our relationship. Not for anyone but me.

When I was twenty-six, I went with my mother to an ashram in the Bahamas. In my memory, it had been life changing, even romantic in its spiritual intensity, and I knew then that someday I would return when I needed to. The Rat Park study is what convinced me that this ashram might be the answer. If anywhere might represent compassion and connection, this place would be it. A self-directed rehab, one designed just for me.

When I began to make serious plans to go back, this time alone, I pulled out photos from my first visit. I was so young and unknowing in those pictures. I had a boyfriend in Portland, one I wasn't terribly into but who would eventually choose a different woman over me. I didn't yet know that in almost twenty years, I'd be replaying the same story, this tiresome story of not being chosen. I would be in therapy through most of those next twenty years. I would write ten books. I would have two beautiful baby boys. I would marry twice. But my wound would stay fresh.

My friends all wanted to get together before I left, because what if they were losing a drinking buddy? I was the kind of friend who never said no. If someone wanted to go out last minute, I got a babysitter. If a friend was in the mood for karaoke tomorrow night, I made it happen. No matter that I had clients the next day or somewhere to be at nine in the morning. I went out, and I stayed out until we closed down the bar. I couldn't imagine who I would become now that I planned to clean up. I had been this person for so long that I didn't remember living any other way.

The night I left for the airport, I smoked one last cigarette and drank half a glass of wine. My efforts to cram in one more of everything didn't even work anymore. I was that ready for a new experience in life. I took a red eye to Atlanta where I changed planes to arrive in Nassau late morning. I was so excited, I barely slept on either flight. I wasn't nervous, exactly, but I was anxious about what to expect, about what kind of transformation I might undergo. I cried a little. Perhaps I was mourning an old life. Perhaps I knew there was no turning back to how I'd been living. I wanted desperately to change my life, and it wasn't just the drinking. I knew that was just a symptom of a larger despair. I wanted my entire life to break open. I wanted to unfold again and again, to soften into something new.

All Sivananda guests arrive at the ashram by boat, which we meet in Nassau. I could feel a flutter in my throat as we docked. One other woman was on the boat with me. She had been at the ashram for a week already and had gone into Nassau for the day. She was in her sixties and single. She told me she came every year on her own, away from the busyness of her life to reconnect with herself. Her story made me hopeful I'd have a similar experience.

The first day, though, after getting settled in my tent, I felt awash with a sense of being an outsider.

I skipped the second morning's yoga and instead woke up in time to eat. I sat with the same women as the day before, and then I spent the day lying on the beach. Perfect yoga-bodied women in bikinis lay on towels near me. Their names were Shanti and Kali. Their names weren't really Shanti and Kali, of course. Their names were Debbie and Cindy, and they lived in Iowa. But I reminded myself to be nice. This was the kind of place Debbie could be Shanti if she wanted. She was surely hoping for her own kind of transformation. The sun warmed my skin, and when I got too hot, I floated for a while in the water. I fell asleep on my towel and woke to a sore butt. Around three o'clock, I ambled back into the lush property of the ashram to change for yoga.

The teacher was an older man. "Yoga is an inner body workout," he told us. "If you're uncomfortable, you stop. Get into child's pose and relax. We'll all laugh at you, but that's okay. If you're enlightened, you won't care."

We laughed. The yoga platform was on the bay and in the distance were the sounds of gulls and motorboats racing by.

"See?" he said. "You're already laughing at yourself. That's a good thing."

Fine. I would laugh at myself. At the end of class, we lay in *savasana*, corpse pose, legs spread, palms up to receive. The teacher explained *savasana* was one of the most challenging yoga poses. He warned us against simply relaxing there or falling asleep as people often seemed to do. Instead, we should focus on the complete release of ego. *Savasana* was about surrender to death. I thought of this often while there. I still think of it now. Our egos are so massive. You can feel yours in corpse pose, how it won't get out of the way, how it holds so tightly to the things it thinks it needs to be okay.

At dinner, I sat again with those same two women.

"How are you liking it so far?" one of them asked.

"I'm getting there," I answered.

After dinner, the thought hit me: *I would love a glass of wine. And a cigarette.* I was well aware that, like my friend told me, I could likely get one about five minutes down the beach at Atlantis. But I didn't want it *that* badly. I wouldn't say I wanted it *badly* at all. I also would have been delighted if a love affair blossomed, which is what I would have longed for in the past. But I didn't feel particularly attached to that thought either. I was sharply aware too that in the past, the desire for a love affair had been steeped in craving, had led to intense restlessness, and was very much tied up with my sense of worth. The drinking wasn't tinged by any of that. In fact, I was shocked by how easily this was going, by how little wine and cigarettes mattered to me now that I was in this setting.

The following day at brunch, I heaped food onto my plate. I wasn't particularly hungry, but when food is available only twice a day and at specific times, it's difficult not to worry about being hungry. Isn't that silly? Yet over time, I noticed that many of the mealtime conversations focused on this conundrum: Do I eat too much now so I won't be hungry later? Or do I eat only until full now and risk being hungry later?

I sat in the same place each meal. I was such a creature of habit. Those other women sat elsewhere now, surely expanding their experience while here. I made a mental note to do the same next meal. This tendency of mine to avoid discomfort, avoid feeling out of place and insecure, was a part of why I was an addict.

Each day was the same. I woke in time for brunch, lay in the sun and swam in the ocean until 3:30 p.m., did afternoon yoga, dinner, and evening *satsang*. I made a few friends, and before my stay was over, I even made a group of friends— funny, interesting, thoughtful people from different parts of the country. We sought each other out at meals and on the beach, and we became close enough that we exchanged phone numbers before they left, since they all left before I did, with a promise we'd meet back there again. I hardly thought about drinking or cigarettes, which fascinated me. I had a vape with me, in case I craved nicotine, but this simply didn't happen, and I didn't pull out the vape once. The concept of Rat Park seemed unlikely, but here I was, in my own lovely rat park, completely disinterested in the substances of my choice.

Men were still on my mind, however, and now that I wasn't anesthetizing myself, the feelings I had about men were rushing to the surface. In my tent, I cried uncontrollably, night after night, feeling for the first time in many months how Bob had treated me all those years, always looking for someone else, never happy with just me. I let him decide I wasn't good enough, and in the process, I had let myself believe I wasn't either. I cried about Kyle, how he left me behind, understandably, when the baby came. I cried about being the one always uncared for, the unloved one, all those old feelings racing through me again. And I cried because I couldn't see how I would ever manage to have love again now that these two men had ruined my spirit and then my heart.

I felt the spread of something, a darkness, a thick,

unmanageable pain, and I covered my mouth so that people in neighboring tents wouldn't hear how hard I cried. The pain from both of those relationships coursed through me like the water in the bay. I couldn't stop it. I was afraid it wouldn't stop. I emailed a friend back in Portland. *I'm afraid no one will ever love me again. I'm afraid I'm unlovable.* I'd been feeling those things for thirty years, and here they were again, as fresh as if they were new. Lucy said this wasn't true. It wasn't the same feeling. We retraced the same path, but it was as though spiraling up a mountain. It was familiar, yes, but it wasn't like before. I wanted to believe her, but in this moment, lying on that hard, single bed, I felt like I had when I was ten and my mother had left, like I was nineteen and had lost my first love to another woman, like I was losing Kyle all over again.

The following morning, though, I was somehow all right again. Feelings do pass, as long as you don't cling too tightly.

By the time I left, after three full weeks, I felt both hesitant and excited. Something had shifted inside me. Before I'd gone, it had seemed too good to hope for, too unlikely. Yet here it was, a new feeling. I knew, though, that things could feel differently back at home, back in my life, where stress lived, where reminders of Kyle were everywhere, where my home and my children and my careers still needed much tending.

I hadn't been sure before, but I now felt confident that I was handling my addictions my own way. I suspected this would anger some people. I had seen the way readers responded to the essay I wrote three years earlier. I had also seen the reactions to Gabrielle Glaser's infamous article in the *Atlantic* in which she shared research suggesting that AA doesn't help as many people as we are led to believe.* People who had been helped through AA were uncompromising in their feelings that Glaser was an asshole. Many, if not most, believe if you drink too much, you need to become sober. Through AA. Period. End of story. When Bob heard of my plans to change my relationship with alcohol on my own terms, he called me an alcoholic, mocked me, and made sure I (and anyone who would listen) knew that this was more evidence of my problem. I'm sure he wasn't the only one who felt this way, but after decades of pissing off people as a writer and maybe thanks to age, I cared a lot less about what others thought.

During my days at the ashram, I had become clear about my plans to moderate when I returned home. Perhaps it was the ashram itself, which is a place rich with tranquility and spirituality, but I could feel that hope like a light inside. It was as though I was getting a sneak peek of my own ability to be happier again. Because there it was, a pulsating sensation, like a promise, at the base of my heart. It felt a lot like happiness. And the feeling suggested to me that I could have this peace at home. I knew things would be different. Home was no spiritual center. But the light was *there*. After all this time, my happiness was still in there, just waiting to reemerge. And this knowledge traveled through my system, making me know that I did not have a disease in my brain. Humans respond to the idea of

Kerry Cohen

---

* Gabrielle Glaser, "The Irrationality of Alcoholics Anonymous," *The Atlantic*, April 2015, https://www.theatlantic.com/magazine/archive /2015/04/the-irrationality-of-alcoholics-anonymous/386255/.

alcoholism as a disease. If *other* people have the disease, then I'm safe. *Other* people have it, but not *me*. I don't buy this idea that alcoholism is a disease at all. I couldn't have gone forty years of my life and then suddenly adopted this disease. It's not like I picked it up from someone who hadn't been washing his hands enough. I didn't get it from having unprotected sex with an alcoholic. Addiction is a spiritual problem, and just like the rats who didn't get to live in Rat Park, most of us have it. We live in a society where the idea of happiness and fulfillment is just out of reach. You can get it if you buy this thing. You can have it if you invest in that. True engagement and connection, with ourselves, with others, with a sense of purpose, is rarely easy to sustain. We'd have to live full time in Rat Park or here at the ashram. Barring that, most of us are going to wind up addicted to something in the hopes that the thing we want—alcohol, drugs, sex, love, gambling, starvation—will raise us out of the despair of living in this world.

When one of my friends was just nineteen, she stayed in a psychiatric hospital, at least partially because she was drinking and drugging too much. She knew what she needed to say and do to get out (this wasn't her first time there), so she did. The day she left, the psychiatrist assigned to her sat her down for a lecture about addiction. He explained how her brain processed her drug use. He described how if she didn't stop all her behaviors, she would wind up miserable and alone, maybe even dead. She nodded, used to these sorts of lectures. He told her nothing she didn't already know. Within a few hours of being out, she went to her favorite strip club. There are tons in

Portland. She got herself a drink and parked herself in front of a slot machine. At some point, she looked to her left, and there was the psychiatrist. He was also in front of a video machine, a drink in one hand, a cigarette in another, two mostly naked women hanging on him. She jokes that had someone brought him a piece of cake right then, he would have yelled, "Hurry! Put it in my mouth!" He looked up, meeting his patient's gaze, and then quickly looked away.

Seventeen

I waited.

WHAT A PERFECT, WELL-ROUNDED, REDEMPTIVE STORY THIS would have been had I come home from the ashram and made good on my promise to myself to maintain a spiritual practice, including yoga. I almost managed to do this. I signed up for yoga classes and took one here and there. I bought some good audio books and made myself take walks. I did other things too. I didn't take up with a new man. I lay in bed with that vape I'd bought and watched Netflix and Hulu. I didn't drink. I noticed things I'd been neglecting inside the house, like the living room, which had been slowly transforming into a sports equipment depository for Griffin. I deep cleaned the kitchen. I played board games with my children. I called a plumber about the bathroom in the basement that had been out of order for the better part of a year.

I cried a lot and too easily.

On my third day home, Kyle sent me a message letting me know he missed me and had a present for me, and could we see each other? I knew intuitively saying yes was a bad idea, but I went to see him the next day. Kyle and his baby and his determination that we be just friends. For the next day and a half, I was destroyed. I didn't drink. I took a long walk, crying the whole time. I went on online dating sites, my own sort of relapse, and managed to only feel worse.

Mostly, I waited. I waited to feel better.

In therapy, I tried to untangle what was inexplicable despair and what was the loneliness I felt without a man in my life, an old explanation on which I had long hung my unhappiness. This was the end of 2016. Icons from my childhood had been dropping off the earth. After eight years with the only president I'd ever loved, a racist misogynist had been voted into office, and he was assigning a whole bunch more racist misogynists to his cabinet. Worse, we couldn't even wish impeachment, because he'd probably for that very reason chosen a vice president who believed the earth was only six thousand years old and that women should be punished for having miscarriages. I knew at least two people who had killed themselves within the past month. The world would keep going like this, it seemed. For so long, I had relied on my sex and love addiction to give me hope that I might feel better. But I no longer wanted to be disappointed. I no longer wanted to feel humiliated. I had harvested all that addiction could do for me, and it didn't work anymore. Nothing worked anymore.

I wish I could say that stopping all my addictions made my life suddenly wonderful, but it was quite the opposite. Everything sucked. I felt stuck, almost frantic. *Get me out of here!* But "here" was simply my life, and I wanted to keep living. I believed with the same foolish hope I had always had that things would get better eventually, that I would feel better about those things. An addict who doesn't reach for his/her addiction is like a bug stuck in a jar. We have two choices: race around in a panic, looking for a nonexistent exit, or stay still. This idea that addicts need to *do* something, go to meetings, go to rehab, work the steps, take classes, exercise, make plans… it all sounded so unnecessary. We don't have to do any of that. We simply have to sit there. I've known so many people—I bet you have too—who spend years, even decades, trying to feel better. They are always running off to acupuncture and yoga and eye movement desensitization and reprocessing (EMDR) and reflexology and Reiki. They take supplements. Their shelves are full of self-help books. But they can't seem to get better, no matter how hard they try.

I waited some more.

Following the first step of moderation management (MM), I was taking the month off from drinking. My friends, eager to support me, worried about drinking or smoking around me, but as long as I had something tasty to drink, such as some kind of sparkling juice, and my vape, I didn't even feel tempted. I planned to break the fast on New Year's Eve at my annual New Year's Eve party. Not that I intended to get drunk, but I hoped to have a couple of glasses of red wine as the night progressed. I was not following MM to the letter. I liked that it existed, as it proved that others had had success with controlling their drinking after a period of feeling out of control, but hard and fast rules rarely worked for me. I planned to loosely follow its tenets, and I would see how that worked for me.

Moderation management has long been controversial. The obvious reason for controversy is that our cultural beliefs about addiction are stuck in the brain disease model. But also, the founder of MM, Audrey Kishline, joined AA, and just a few months later, she killed two people in a drunk-driving accident. MM understands not everyone will be able to moderate, and those who fail at moderate drinking will need to abstain, but many argue that even suggesting moderation as an option is dangerous for those who need to stop drinking, especially because there is so much shame around addiction. I would argue that most people don't even know about moderation. The pressure from AA and the notion that alcoholism is a disease is strong enough to keep people away. I also know one's ability to be able to moderate or not will show up quickly. In a listserv I joined for those doing moderation management, a couple of the people in the group determined it just wasn't working for them, and they needed to become sober.

Maybe I'm wrong, but I believe people deserve options. More than that, we deserve to know the truth. There are plenty of studies: women are more likely than men to be able to moderate. People in stable socioeconomic situations are more likely to be able to moderate. Heavy drinkers are rarely alcoholics. The assumption that people who shouldn't drink will use any excuse to keep drinking seems patronizing. One of my friends who is in AA told me, "Everyone has to finish their drinking," just like I had to finish my relationship with Bob. On my own terms, and of my own will.

I thought often about whether moderating was even worth it. Why not just quit drinking for good? But I love good wine, and I love knowing why it's good. I have a fantasy that someday, I'll travel to Europe and study wine. I love the light, pleasant feel of a glass of wine or two in my body. I don't like how it feels beyond that. I wanted to get back to *that* relationship to wine.

On New Year's Eve, I had my annual party. I drank a couple glasses of wine, and then I drank nonalcoholic sparkling cider for the rest of the night.

Hannah said, "You're kind of boring now."

I knew she was teasing, but I guess I was. To some extent, I *felt* boring, and for the first time in a long while, that was okay with me. I was…uncomfortable, but I was okay.

Lucy reminded me that discomfort was simply neurons firing in new ways. When your neurons fire the same way again and again, they create a habit, right? Having them fire somewhere new, creating a new pathway and a new habit, is uncomfortable. We tend to think of discomfort as a sign that something is *wrong*, but it's just…different.

At the grocery store, I watched myself pass the wine aisle. There was a subtle pressure, perhaps the ghost effect of those old neural pathways, to buy wine, but I didn't want any, so I walked on. One night, I shared a bottle with a friend. We drank all but a glass's worth, and that amount sat in the bottle next to my bed for a full week before I thought to drink it with another friend. That hadn't happened since before I met Bob.

When I went out, which was now only about once or twice a week, I ordered a glass of wine, usually two, and I savored the taste. I no longer thought about how I could escape so I could drink that wine with a cigarette. I drank it in small, precious sips, enjoying what I had long missed about wine: its body and flavor, and yes, the light, floaty feeling of just a glass or two in my blood. I focused on the conversation at the table, the person in front of me. My mind was no longer split—partly on the person I was with and partly on the next drink, the next cigarette, or the men in the room.

My relationship to men was changing too. I felt comfortable being single. Sort of. That was coming more slowly. I was sometimes anxious for their attention and went to online dating sites. But when I dated those men, I had no need for more than whatever happened organically, which was rarely much of anything. I often felt like I was watching myself from afar. Who was this new woman? I had no idea yet, but she seemed awfully healthy, and I kind of liked her.

My therapist wasn't convinced. Lucy doubted anyone could moderate alcohol, and she admitted she expected me to fall back into heavy drinking. I listened to her arguments, but I was clear. As far as I could tell, I didn't need to quit drinking. I didn't even think about it that much. My plan had been to follow moderation management's guidelines and to use their online support group, but I didn't. That's partly due to being lazy and partly because I forgot. When I told a sober friend about this, he said if he defaulted to laziness, he'd be a full-on drunk. For him, drinking was what he did when he wasn't being vigilant. For me, drinking only happened now when I thought to do so.

Maybe this *is* irresponsible. Maybe I shouldn't be sharing this story in which I learned I could moderate alcohol after a long period of drinking too much. Maybe I shouldn't assume that everyone knows there are many people who can't moderate, people who lose their lives to beer and whisky, who avoid everything and everyone until they wind up alone and in trouble and unable to cope. My sober friends know this to be true about themselves. There is no value in even considering whether they could drink without consequence, though they may have those thoughts here and there.

Life is fucking complicated. So are we. That's why I'm sharing this story.

I didn't quit drinking, but I quit being a lush.

Eighteen

I don't buy wine much.

EVENTUALLY, I FUCKED UP. I HAD TRIED TO REMOVE KYLE from my life, but one night, he asked to see me, and I said yes, and we accidentally had sex. I know, I'm still an asshole! But if my core addiction is love and sex and Kyle was my drug, can you see how this might begin a swirling in my brain like a whirlpool? Everything else drew near the eddy and was pulled under, swallowed whole.

The following morning, I told myself it was fine, no big deal, so what? I slept with Kyle again. That didn't mean anything. I'd erase it from my mind. I called some friends. I talked about how empowered I felt, how he didn't have control over me anymore. I was a badass. I was the single one, dating numerous men. He was stuck at home in his marriage. I was *fine*. I was better than fine. I was strong.

That night, I consulted a psychic, which was the first sign that I might not be fine.

The following night, I felt the pressure like a wide hand on my chest. A drink. I needed to drink. I drove to the closest 7-Eleven. It had been so long since I'd last gone. Without the need for cigarettes and the purple bottle-and-a-half of Bandit I'd bought nightly, I had no reason to be there. But here I was again. I stepped into the fluorescent lights, followed a well-worn path to the shelf of wine. I studied my options and chose the Black Box carton of merlot that holds three glasses' worth. I didn't recognize the clerk.

I poured myself a glass and got into bed. I wished so much I could smoke. I wished so much I could do my old dance of drinking and smoking in the garage while I watched something on Netflix so I could escape myself. But I didn't smoke anymore, and the drag I had tried from a friend's cigarette a few weeks earlier had tasted gross. It was over. My ability to escape into wine and cigarettes was history, and I felt immense grief about that. I wanted so badly to stop this feeling, this awful, sad, useless feeling I had for Kyle. He wasn't mine, and he wouldn't be mine, and that was that. I drank that glass and about half of another glass, and then I willed myself to sleep.

The following morning, I felt just as bad, but I wasn't hungover, which—drinkers so often forget—makes us feel much worse emotionally than we did when we drank to numb our pain. I forced myself out of bed, moved through the day, and gradually, I felt better.

I wish I could provide some fascinating information about relapse and relapse prevention, but there's nothing that interesting to note. It's hard to stick to plans. It's hard to make your brain do something it hasn't done for a long time. We think of conquering addictions as just stopping the behavior, but there are some addictions that don't work like that. Sex and love. Eating. Those of us with process addictions like these can't just avoid our drug of choice. We need love. And sex. And food. We simply need to relate to them in less harmful ways. Because I'm a sex and love addict, I am constantly having to find ways to tangle with my drug of choice without hurting myself or others. I fail a lot. But I keep working on it, because I don't want to live without sex or love. I spent a lot of time wondering about this same approach with alcohol, especially in my case. There seems to be plenty of judgment about moderating alcohol, but no one judges people who try to moderate sex and love.

Moderating sex and love in my life meant limiting the fantasy that sex and love would fill me. Neither would remove my pain, and men wouldn't solve my problems. Perhaps I could take the same approach with wine. A bottle of malbec wouldn't release me from the ways in which my heart hurt, from the fact that my career hadn't become what I'd wanted, from the grief that always hovered in the background because my son was autistic. Having fun helped. Adventure and genuine intimacy cut into the mundane. But nothing in that wineglass would save me from my chronic condition of being human.

Here's what I do: I don't buy wine much. When I do, if it stays in my house, I make sure it lasts a good week. Or I save it to share with a friend. When I go out, I do not drink more than two or three glasses of wine, and three is only after much consideration. I do not budge on these rules.

I lost fifteen pounds in the first couple of months. As annoyed with myself as I am with the immense appeal of this cultural trap, it helps.

My skin looks and feels better, and I worry less about wrinkles.

I am saving close to $300 per month by not buying wine.

I feel less foggy most days, although I do feel foggy a lot. I think that's just middle age.

I don't tell everyone about my changed relationship to drinking and smoking, just in case everything becomes horrible and there is literally nothing left to live for and I want to go back to being a drunk.

One of my clients noted how often her friends act weird when she takes time off from drinking. Or refuses dessert. Or otherwise takes care of herself. As much as we women like to make noise about supporting one another, when one of us is doing something we figure we should be doing too, we can feel bad about ourselves.

My friend texted me at ten on a Wednesday night: Want to go do karaoke?

She knew who she was texting. Just a few months earlier, I was the go-to friend for such an impulse. I was always up for anything. On any normal Wednesday night, I was in my garage or backyard or on my front stoop, drinking from a box, smoking, watching a show on my phone. I was *waiting* for the opportunity to get into something. But now, I was already in my pajamas in bed.

I wrote back: Already in bed. I have a full work day tomorrow. Now that I'm not drinking and smoking like an insane person, I know that would be a bad idea for me. And I lost fifteen pounds to boot!

She wrote: No need to get sanctimonious.

It might be easier to be sober where alcohol is concerned. But even if I become sober someday, which I might decide I need to do, I will never be able to be abstain from love and sex, so I'll never be safe from addiction. As I write this, I can promise you that I have already screwed up at least five more times with men. I slept with one only because I wanted to escape myself that night, and then that dude treated me like shit. Another one chose some other woman over me, and I went to all those familiar feelings about how I'm not lovable and blah blah blah. It is possible I will never be free of these feelings. I will keep thinking I've negotiated a new layer of the addiction and then wind up back at what feels like square one. Love and sex are my true addictions, and because I can't leave them behind like substance abusers can with their drug of choice, I will probably spend my life trying to find a balance with them that doesn't make me feel like shit.

I don't have that problem with wine.

The narrative of addiction is always the same: I loved the thing to which I was addicted, I did horrible things, and it

almost killed me or someone else, and finally, I was redeemed.
What if I have a different story to tell? What if your resistance
to that unusual story isn't because it's *wrong* but because it's
uncomfortable...because it's different?

Nineteen

I smile hello.

IN OKLAHOMA, AT THE RESIDENCY WHERE I TEACH, I LAY in bed in my hotel room watching reality TV instead of all the things I used to do when there. Normally, during the residency, I was busy partying. Everyone knew to come to my room. There would be alcohol. There would be a smoking balcony. There would be fun. So much of this changing behavior stuff is figuring out how to replace the behavior that took up so much of your time before. I replaced it with hiding in my hotel room. I took a seven-mile walk one day, just to keep moving. Otherwise, I lay in bed. On television, a commercial kept airing: a man talked about being an addict and getting help. A woman said she was an alcoholic. And then a white man with glasses and a stethoscope said,

"Addiction is a disease. What are you waiting for? You need professional help."

The commercial was offensive and condescending, and I wanted to throw something at the television every time it came on. But it was also a good reminder to hold my shit together and not fall into old habits while there. At every residency since the MFA program's inception, I had been engaged in some sort of drama, usually involving Bob. This was the first time I was there with no man drama, no boyfriend or husband, period. There I was in my hotel room bed watching *Sister Wives*, which glamorized polygamy, and another show about former sister wives saving sister wives from their oppressed, miserable lives. I had two nights in which I monitored myself and limited my wine intake, and then I got sick. It started with a stomach virus, one of the worst I've ever had (the pain was bad enough that I wondered whether I should go to the hospital), and when that abated, I had an evil flu, merciless enough that I spent the remaining six days of the residency under the covers and alone.

At least I didn't have to think about how to change my behavior while there. That was another gift, I suppose. Thanks a whole hell of a lot.

I traveled home still sick and got right back into my own bed. I went back to waiting to feel better. Sometimes I even did. Feel better, that is.

I don't know if things get better. I hope they do. I'm still in my forties. People tell me that your fifties are the best. So are your sixties. I try not to freak out about these numbers.

Spring came this year to Portland. It comes every year of course, but that's good to remember. When it came this time, it did so with a glory we hadn't seen in years, because we got more rain than usual in the winter. Pale-pink cherry blossoms, jasmine, blue hydrangea, sconce-sized magnolias blooming from trees. The waterfront lined with those flowering trees like a chorus. It is so lush. The world can be so goddamn beautiful.

The smell of spring reminds me of when I first met Kyle, that rush of desire and exhilaration. The sweet promise of my core addiction: that somehow a man will make me better. The sad loss of that hope is still there too.

I take walks through the beauty of this spring. I have to exercise! I have to take care of myself, even when I don't want to, which is most of the time. It is so hard to find that balance between wanting and doing and deciding how much to force myself and how much to allow my natural physical state, which is passivity. I have work I should be doing too. I have students who expect feedback and this book to write and the next book I want to write. But I make myself go. I pass neighbors with strollers and husbands. I walk past the local bar, some old familiar faces, still on the benches outside with their pints of beer and cigarettes. Other neighbors on runs, checking their watches to see how much longer until they've completed their goal. We smile hello.

Reading Group Guide

1. Kerry writes, "Addiction specialists say that everyone has either a problematic relationship to alcohol, a controlled relationship to alcohol, or no relationship to alcohol." What is your relationship to alcohol? Has it changed over time? Why do you think that is?

2. Kerry makes clear that prior to this time in her life, she hadn't been a drinker, and she believed this might be evidence that she could someday have a normal relationship to alcohol again. Do you agree? Why or why not?

3. Throughout the book, Kerry notes that it's women, especially middle-aged women, who seem to be drinking more. Why do you think this might be?

4. Kerry notes that the story she tells about Bob is simply the "she said" part of what happened. Can there be more than one story? Is one story more "true" than another?

5. Kerry writes about addiction as resembling a balloon that bulges out with other types of addictions when one is pushed down. Do you have a "balloon" of addictions? What's inside your balloon?

6. Kerry came to believe that her drinking was a symptom of her real addiction—sex and love. What do you think about this?

7. The Rat Park study by Bruce Alexander is described on page 153–154. How does this study apply to your life or to people you know?

8. Kerry references Lidia Yuknavitch's quote "I'm not the story you made of me," talking about the way we make sense of our lives. What stories do you have about yourself? Are they yours, or were they made up about you by others? By society?

9. Kerry writes of addiction, "It is a deeply layered spiritual problem. It is a human problem." Discuss this idea.

10. Life did not suddenly get better after Kerry stopped drinking heavily. If you are in recovery from an addiction, what was your experience? What did you think was going to happen versus what *actually* happened?

A Conversation with the Author

What is a lush? Do you still see yourself as one?

My intention in using this word as a title went beyond its basic definition of "a person who drinks too much." I wanted to capture its other meaning, the one that describes fullness and abundance. One of the main concepts I hoped to explore in the book is middle age, that sense when you reach about forty, you look around at your life and think, *Really? This is my life?* There's a sense, perhaps especially for women, that life will be rich and fulfilling if you follow the rules, i.e., get married, have babies, and perhaps have a career. During the time I wrote about in the book, my life was lush. It was insanely lush! I had my two children, one with special needs, three careers, and a new blended family. I'd had some success as an author. And, yet, there I was—not terribly happy. In my mind, the excessive drinking to avoid this existential angst was what made me a lush. I drank too much amid a very full life that should have been more satisfying than it was.

Why did you write this book?

I wrote this book for the same reason I wrote all the memoirs I've written. I wanted to understand what had happened in my life. I wanted to make meaning out of a time in my life that would otherwise feel meaningless. I write memoir out of the desperate need to keep my life from sinking into pointlessness. That's the main reason. I was completely confused as to why I was suddenly drinking way too much after a life of having no relationship to drinking. Even more concerning, when I looked around, it seemed that almost every middle-aged woman I knew or met was drinking too much as well. I wanted to understand why, both for me and for them.

How does it feel to discuss your frailties and mistakes so openly?

Honestly, I wish I knew a different way to be! I have always been like that, whether as a writer or a friend. How does it feel? It feels authentic. It feels honest. It feels freeing. It also leads to being easily hurt by people though. Memoir writers *have* to do that. We have to show our asses. We have to take responsibility for ourselves in the world. As a result, though, people have historically been really mean to memoir writers! Especially women. I've thought about that often. Memoirs often show people truths about themselves they don't like, so

Kerry Cohen

there's a lot of projection out there. It's worse for women, I think, because we are the world's scapegoats. Additionally, it makes some people very angry when women have the gall to speak up. Just look to history for evidence of that. Women's voices are degraded, shushed, twisted, and censored. There aren't tons of safe places for us to claim words.

So, to get back to the question, discussing the truth about myself—all my flaws and scars and bruises—feels fantastic. It's the repercussions for doing so that doesn't always feel that great.

You write about our cultural conversation around women and wine, which is often humorous and chummy. How has your perception of the way we view female drinking changed, as your own relationship to alcohol has changed?

Like anything you notice more, I've become much warier of the conversation. Suggesting women could use some cocktails to deal with life is not the problem. The problem is the silence about *why* we need those cocktails. Like most things in our culture concerning women, we've made the conversation into something cutesy and fun rather than talking about what's really going on. And what's really going on is that it's hard to be a woman! Look at the statistics. We still get paid less than men. We are sexually harassed and assaulted and then blamed for it. We are never pretty enough or thin enough. And then we lose even more power as we age. I sound so negative! Obviously there have been some positive developments. My point is only that it makes a lot of sense to me why wine is marketed to women. I just wish we'd talk more honestly about why.

How do you feel about the pervasiveness of alcohol as a basic ingredient of female friendships?

My feelings are similar to the ones I expressed answering the previous question. Marketing alcohol to women in ways that feel chummy and light is part of the way our patriarchal, capitalist system distracts women, and everyone else, from the ways in which women are subjugated. I mean, obviously I've been a part of this problem. My friends and I still drink together rather than, say, get the feminist revolution started. And there is a way it *still* feels like we deserve to have a glass or two of wine while we catch each other up on our lives and complain about our kids or men or ways we get treated because we're women. The key seems to stay conscious of what's really happening regarding how we're using alcohol. Are we relaxing together? Or, are we neglecting ourselves and the people we love?

How have you dealt with people who did not agree with your method of handling your relationship with alcohol?

I don't deal with them. I feel confident about my approach. Like I noted in the book, I may still someday decide I need to abstain, but for now moderation continues to work. It seems obvious to me that if other people have issues with my decision, that's more about them than me. I take no issue with other people's decisions regarding their recovery, and I would hope other people will grant me the same. I realize it was a risk to write about it. A few people think I was irresponsible to do so, that it would somehow encourage other people to keep drinking when they needed to stop. I don't agree. Moderation is one option, and it can be just as viable as quitting, depending on the situation. I'm aware my belief system around addiction might be different from many others, though. I believe in harm reduction perhaps more than I believe in abstinence. People who have addictions, no matter what those addictions are, are hurting in some way. Sometimes that hurt is existential. Sometimes it's due to trauma. Whatever the reason, taking away the drug or behavior won't solve the real problem. As I say in the book, addiction is a spiritual problem, and the spiritual problem is one pretty much all of us have.

Lush shares some similarities with your first memoir, _Loose Girl_, although they are very different. How did your writing experiences of the two memoirs differ?

In lots of ways, _Loose Girl_ is simpler because I understood less about my addiction then. And, _Loose Girl_ is more about being a girl growing up in this culture than it is about sex and love addiction. As I've gotten older, everything seems more complicated and certainly less containable. That's the main way it was different. I wrote _Loose Girl_ after I had lived those years, while I started writing _Lush_ while I was still inside them. Also, there were lots more voices in my ear writing _Lush_. _Loose Girl_ was my first memoir, while _Lush_ is my fourth. Certain people were upset about being written about this time. I almost didn't get the book written, to be honest. But, in the eleventh hour, I reunited with a friend who I'd lost because of that person who tried to keep *Lush* from happening, and she did some kind of magic that helped turn *Lush* into what it is now. So, *Loose Girl* was a joy to write, while writing this one was drama-filled, tear-filled, and basically almost killed me!

What's next for you?

I'm working on my first adult novel. (Taking a break from memoir for now!) That's been an exciting and challenging project. I probably shouldn't say anything because what if it doesn't work and then I've said this thing and now you'll all know that I failed! I will say that I'm working with an unreliable female narrator, which is a concept I'm more and more fascinated with, especially as we're beginning to look at how often we don't believe, or even blame, women in our culture for their own victimizations.

Acknowledgments

I should write "Laurel Hermanson" three hundred times. I should sing her name in the voice of a sparrow. I should hire one of those fancy airplanes to write her name in the sky. If I was into women, even just a little bit, I would ask that lady to marry me. I know writers say "this book wouldn't have happened if it weren't for…" all the time, but that is truly the case here. This book was in shambles. It was garbage. Calling it a book would have been generous. In the eleventh hour, Laurel asked to see it. She looked over the material and said, "I know what we need to do." Then, she performed magic. I still don't understand how she pulled this off.

There were other people involved of course. They, too, deserve their names sung. Thank you, Rayhané Sanders, who, in our very first dance together, had to go through hell, and who fought like a bear for me. I promise we will have smoother sailing going forward. Shana Drehs, my editor, who believed enough in the potential of my story to take a chance. Cassie Gutman, Bret Kehoe, Adrienne Krogh, Danielle McNaughton, Irene O'Brien, and Liz Kelsch—thank you for making this the best book it could be.

I have immense appreciation for my friends who have walked with me through it all. There are many of you, but I'd be remiss to not name Jennifer Martz, Lesley Harper, and Julie Swenson. My sister, Tyler Cohen, is a gem. My mother and stepfather are swell. And Daddy, I hope you will forgive me for really raking you over the coals in this one. There's a reason you said, "No more memoirs!" Sorry, but I probably have a couple more in me.

Big thanks to Michael for sticking by me through all my bad choices. To another certain someone I love, who has indeed been one of those bad choices. You know who you are.

And my children, who…actually, they didn't do anything to help with this book! I don't remember getting any notes from those two. They didn't even proofread. Four and a half days of labor between the two of them, and this is what I get! Just kidding, my loves. You two are my absolute everythings.

About the Author

PHOTO © KERRY COHEN

KERRY COHEN is the author of the memoirs *Loose Girl: A Memoir of Promiscuity*, *Seeing Ezra: A Mother's Story of Autism, Unconditional Love, and the Meaning of Normal*, and *Girl Trouble*, as well as many other fiction and nonfiction books. Her work has been featured in the *New York Times* and the *Washington Post*, and she has been a guest on *Dr. Phil*, *Good Morning America*, and the BBC's *Saturday Live*. Her story was also featured on WE Network as part of the documentary *The Secret Lives of Women*.

She is a doctor of clinical psychology and works as a licensed therapist in Portland, Oregon.